Mark Moore

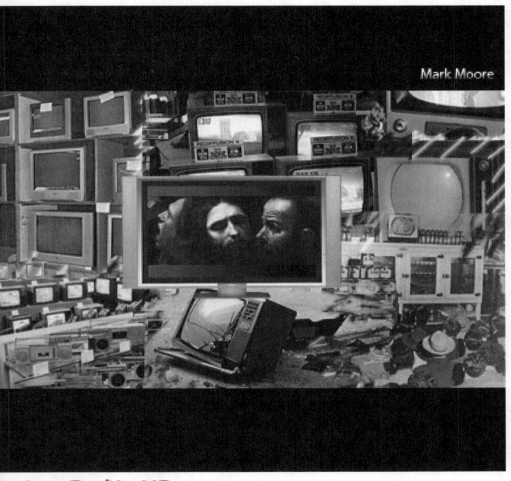

eeing God in HD

Library of Congress Cataloging-in-Publication Data

Moore, Mark E. (Mark Edward), 1963-
  Seeing God in HD : God's word in today's world / by Mark E. Moore.
     p. cm.
  ISBN 978-0-89900-930-8 (hardback)
  1. Bible–Hermeneutics. I. Title.
  BS476.M59 2008
  220.601–dc22

                                              2007045632

To *Willard Black,*
founder of *The Institute for Christian Resources*

&

To *Shane Wood,*
the future of *The Institute for Christian Resources*

That you two are the bookends for this present journey
gives me more joy than my words can adequately express.

Preface

B iblical illiteracy has reached epidemic proportions even within the sanctuary of God's church. In a recent survey, many Americans were convinced that Joan of Arc was Noah's wife and the Epistles were the spouses of the Apostles. Most have no clue that the Bible contains 66 books in 3 languages spanning 1400 years. Ten out of ten people cannot even find the book of Hezekiah . . . and if you wonder why, you might just be part of the problem. Our airwaves are littered with misinformation about the Bible and no small dose of outright heresy. What's worse, most Christ followers have little ability to distinguish truth from error because they are only vaguely familiar with the Word of God.

If the Bible really is the revelation of God, this appalling ignorance will inevitably have detrimental effects on the Church. How will Christians discover and implement their spiritual gifts if they are not grounded in the Word? How will beleaguered spiritual warriors send the enemy into retreat apart from the Sword of Scripture? How will shepherds feed their flocks without the meaty doctrines of the Bible? Our assemblies are bloated with the cotton candy of pop-psychology that so tickles itching ears.

We have mastered the mass assembly with seeker-sensitive sermons and clever marketing strategies. Don't get me wrong, this is fantastic progress for evangelism. And frankly, if one had to choose between evangelism and edification, one should prioritize lost sheep over emaciated sheep every time. At the same time, there is no necessary reason for making such a choice given the informational and technological advances the Lord has graciously put at our disposal. That's what this book is all about. We want to offer you the methods of interpretation through technologically available information. In other words, this book will give you a college-level course in *How to Interpret the Bible* using nothing but your own Bible and free internet resources.

Clarification: It is not the goal of this book to tell you what the Bible says. Rather, the goal of this book is to provide you with the tools and information to enable you to determine for yourself how to read, interpret, apply, and communicate God's message in Scripture. It would be difficult to overstate the excitement I feel at this moment as the author of such a work. After seventeen years of teaching at Ozark Christian College, I can tell you with confidence that this course has made more of an impact than anything I've ever taught. There is no question that other courses can deeply move students as they look at the biblical text under the guidance of a studied 'rabbi.' But enabling students to discover *for themselves* the hidden treasures of Scripture is a liberating and exhilarating exercise. Confidence in reading and understanding God's Word is a priceless gift which will increase in value each time you share it. Enjoy the journey; responsibly execute the trust.

Mark E. Moore

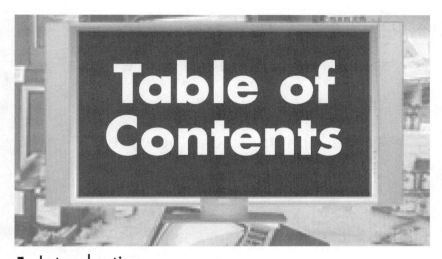

Table of Contents

Appendixes

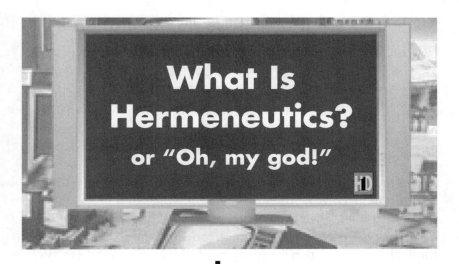

What Is
Hermeneutics?
or "Oh, my god!"

I f you are really interested in Bible interpretation you will pay attention to two gods. Obviously Yahweh is the author of the book(s) that so captures our devotion. Yet there is another god (lower case 'g') that captures our imagination. He was a winged imp named Hermes, a favorite of orators and poets, travelers and merchants, thieves and liars. Why? Because of his skills in both travel and speech. You can recognize him by his winged feet which carried him from the Pantheon of the gods to mortal realms. When Zeus, or some other notable deity, had a message for humans, Hermes was his herald. He  had no choice but to carry the message of his superiors; however, he loved to play the trickster, giving the right message with the wrong implication. He entertained himself by purposefully deceiving his 'clients.' It was from this messenger god that Bible interpretation got its formal name: 'hermeneutics' (though we certainly have no intentions of twisting the message as he did). Simply put, *hermeneutics is the art and science of interpretation.*

The Science of Bible Interpretation

What you are about to study is a science. It is not a 'hard' science that can be reduced to test tubes and element charts. Rather it is a science of language—specifically, how language works. Language has rules, you know—rules about words, grammar, history, and logic. If you look back at the table of contents of this book you will notice the major subjects we will investigate: The rules of *literary* and *historical* context; rules for defining *words* and understanding *grammar*; rules for *parallel* passages and appropriate *applications*; as well as rules for reading specific *genres* (categories) of biblical literature—psalms, gospels, history, prophecy, etc. *Who makes up these rules? No one and everyone.* It's not like a bunch of theologians sneaked off to some cathedral in the Alps and came down with a list of divine hermeneutical 'do's' and 'don'ts.' These rules come from observing how language actually works in the rough and tumble of real life. They are observations about the language of the marketplace and the blog, the sitcom and comedy central. This is why we can say that hermeneutics is truly a science—it comes from observing this incredibly complex and eminently fascinating phenomenon we call 'language.'

> *Hermeneutics is the science of the way language actually works in everyday life.*

> **Caution:**
> *The scientific rules of Hermeneutics will not tell you what every difficult passage means but it will help you know what it can not mean.*

The Art of Bible Interpretation

Hermeneutics, however, is more than scientific rules; it requires a good bit of artistic skill. For example, if one of your friends says, "What a fox!" You may not know precisely what this means without the help of your inner artist. After all, if you are a guy and another guy says this about some cute girl at school, you probably understand him to mean that she is 'hot' (not thermally) or a 'babe' (not chronologically) or a 'knockout' (not medically). On the other hand, if he says this about one of your guy friends he probably means he is sly. On the other hand, if you are out hunting deer and your dad says "What a fox!" he is probably talking about an actual mammalian quadruped of the canine genus. In other words, *language is slippery.* Imagine the poor foreign exchange student whom you happily greet: "What's up?" She looks to the sky for the answer, so you say, "No, I mean 'what's going down.'" She drops her gaze to the ground, so you say, "What's going on?" "On what?" she asks. All this leads me to believe that English is the world's most popular language partially because it is so easy to speak badly. (We do have a confusing language, indeed, when something that is 'hot' can also be 'cool'; where boxing rings are square; where you park in a driveway and drive in a parkway; and restrooms are the last place you actually want to rest.)

Mastering language is one of the most interesting and exhausting tasks of human life. Literalistic rules just won't cut it. For example, one time I was in Mexico drinking a Coke. I wanted to offer a 'sip' to the missionary's daughter (read here an appropriate sigh from a teenager pining over a lovely Latina). My Spanish was pretty pathetic, but I wanted to give it a try. I knew how to say, "Do you want"—"¿Quieres?" And I knew the verb "to drink"—"beber." I even knew how to put a diminutive ending onto a word to make it mean "small"—"ito." So my sentence came out, "¿Quieres un bebito?" The problem is, of course, that this does NOT mean, "Do you want a drink?" it means "Do you want a baby"!!! Like I said, mere rules are insufficient. It takes both the rules of linguistic science as well as the interpretive artist. Yet consider this: human beings are the only animals that use language. Oh, I know about Koko the gorilla who uses simple sign language, and the moans of whales (I even have a new age CD of whales on my iPod). But to compare this with the abstract concepts of human language is like comparing an inadvertent belch with a Mozart sonata just because both started in the key of 'C.' What we do as humans is more than complex, it is more than extraordinary; it is nothing less than a spiritual activity, for this is an attribute that we share with God and his angels to which no other animal can stake a claim.

> *Language is an expression of our **Imago Dei**.*

The Simplicity and Complexity
of Human Language

All human communication consists of three elements: the *author*, the *text* (written, oral, or visual), and the *interpreter*(s).[1] It is that simple. Now, let's illustrate how it works. *Written Texts:* As you read this book, three elements are involved: The author (yours truly), a printed text which you hold in your hand, and a reader (the possessor of said hands). *Audio texts:* If you listen to the radio, there is a singer or DJ who produces certain sounds, these sounds are transmitted through a radio signal, and listeners receive and interpret the sounds. *Visual texts:* If a traffic light goes haywire and a police officer waves his hands wildly, the drivers must see and interpret the actions. Summary: it doesn't matter if the particular kind of communication is written, oral, or visual, it will always have an author, the text, and the interpreter. That seems simple enough.

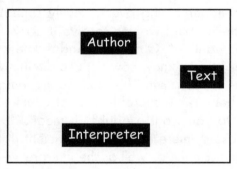

Here is where language gets more complicated, as well as more interesting. The authors are neither robots nor Mr. Spock (except, of course, in the unfortunate situation where you really are named 'Spock'). Authors have both emotions and experiences. What that means is that if a speaker/writer is to be clearly understood, the listener/reader must know something of her

---

[1] In each chapter you can view PowerPoint slides that correspond with the text of the book. These can be found at http://markmoore.org/classes/principles/ or http://collegepress.com/SeeingGod/. For this chapter, click on the PowerPoint button and open the first introductory PowerPoint. Scroll down to the screen that says "Three Elements of Interpretation."

background. Let's say you hear someone give a talk about forgiveness. Do you suppose it would make a difference in how you listened to that person if he was a victim of child abuse, or a survivor of a Nazi concen-

> *All language acts come prepackaged with the author's point of view.*

tration camp, an adulterer, or a theologian? The illustrations here could go on endlessly but surely you get the point: *If you are to fully understand the author's words you must know something of the author's experiences and emotions.*

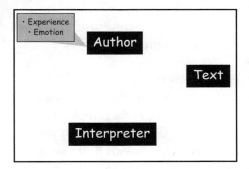

Likewise, every reader/listener has certain experiences, emotions, levels of interest, intelligence, and vocabulary which enables her to a greater or lesser degree to understand an author. If you are into sports, for example, a basketball commentator who uses terms like 'downtown,' 'on fire,' 'zone,' or 'defense' makes great sense to you. For a fireman or a political analyst these same terms are loaded with very different meanings. Or again, the way a divorcee reads the words 'honor your husband' would be quite different than a thirteen-year-old boy, a preacher, or a marriage counselor. Each of us brings our personal history to the text. Our

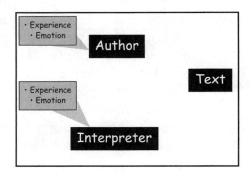

age, race, religion, political affiliation, hobbies, and health all serve to shape our 'listening' of any text, whether it is written, oral, or visual. An inner-city African American in the South may well view a college education, bankers, policemen, or the White House very differently than an Asian-American family in Seattle.

The Plot Thickens: All communication acts are filtered through language which is always an imperfect science (and art). There are pitfalls all along the way.

Pitfall #1: Written texts lose the advantage of vocal inflection (although bold print and italics help with modern texts). We often have to guess at someone's meaning. For example, in John 14:1b the NIV has Jesus saying, "Trust in God; trust also in me." Both phrases are interpreted as commands. But what if we read the first phrase as a simple statement? It would come out: "You trust in God; you *should* trust in me also." Or perhaps we could read the first phrase as a rhetorical question with an obviously affirmative answer: "You trust in God? *Well, then* trust also in me." These other readings are perfectly acceptable grammatically. Contextually these alternate interpretations make a great deal of sense considering

This principle is similar to the Rorschach Test used by some psychiatrists to determine a person's overall composite. What do you see?

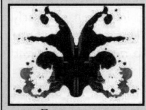

For more see:
http://www.inkblottestwallpaper.com/

Jesus is about to say, "If you have seen me you have seen the Father!" The problem is we can only know the correct interpretation by listening to Jesus' vocal inflection which was lost approximately 2,000 years ago.

Pitfall #2: Nobody is a perfectly clear communicator. Sometimes stuff just comes out badly. Here is an actual announcement from a church paper: "For those of you who have children and don't know it, we have a nursery downstairs." How about this one? "Bertha Belch, a missionary from Africa, will be speaking tonight at Calvary Methodist. Come hear Bertha Belch all the

Misspeaks can be embarrassing. Check these out:

Dinner special — Turkey $2.35; Chicken or Beef $2.25; Children $2.00

Used Cars: Why go elsewhere to be cheated? Come here first.

Auto-Repair Service: Free pick-up and delivery. Try us once, you'll never go anywhere again.

Now is your chance to get your ears pierced and get an extra pair to take home, too.

way from Africa." Now all of us know that everyone misspeaks at times. If we are to be courteous listeners, this will require giving others the benefit of the doubt as we try to understand what they *meant* to say, not just what is written on the page. Political commentators (such as Rush Limbaugh or Tim Russert) are often more interested in using people's words against them than listening sympathetically with the purpose of understanding the author's intended meaning.

Pitfall #3: Translations from one language to another often have difficulty capturing the meaning of a phrase. Why, for example, does Jesus say God 'loves' sinners (Matt 4:44-45) when the Psalms say, "God hates sinners" (Ps 11:5). Is God schizophrenic? For us the terms of 'love' and 'hate' are emotional terms that imply how one feels. For the Hebrew they were descriptions of how one *treated* the other person. So God can provide sunshine and rain for sinners and then turn around and punish them for their evil— he both loves and hates them with his actions. In the same vein, Jesus said we must *hate* our parents or we cannot be his disciples. It is not that we *feel* antipathy for them, but Jesus calls us to leave our homes and families to follow him, and in any Middle-Eastern home that action can only be understood as 'hateful.' Some things just don't translate well.

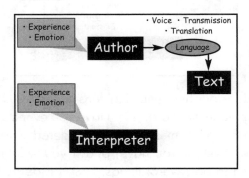

What you fish with will determine what you catch. Or to put it another way, some people wear 3-D glasses and others wear rose-colored lenses. OK, enough with the metaphors, here's what I mean. Some people see the Bible as a history book, and so they find in it historical data. Others see it as a storybook and find helpful moral lessons from fables. Some see it as an ethics text-

> *What you bring to the text will largely determine what you take away from the text.*

book and walk away with rules and doctrines. Still others see it as a quasi-magical book or a lucky rabbit's foot and seek power or mystical comfort from reading it. What you look for is likely what you will find. Let me illustrate how this works. Come with me to the world of romance. Let's say 'girl A' dumps some sorry chump because he is a loser, and 'girl B' adopts him as a lovable 'project.' Girl A sees an immature, selfish pig. The new 'sweetie'—girl B—sees a vulnerable, good-hearted man with potential if she can just love him through this tough spot (oy veh!). It's kind of like that with the Bible. The hermeneutical lens you wear when you approach the Bible will largely determine what you see in it. If you want to see a Jesus who is a middle-class white Republican, you can find him there. If you want to find a reason to criticize God's actions as unjust, you can find it there. If you want to find proof-texts for the liberation of women, just dig a bit, it's there.

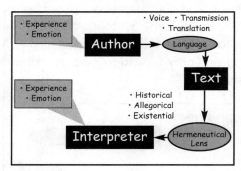

Not only does our hermeneutical lens separate us from the text, so does our hermeneutical distance. Have you ever stared deep into the eyes of an Egyptian mummy and wondered what his life must have been like? Well, if you have, and if you wanted to find out, you would need to do several things. First, (aside from inventing a time machine) you would have to cross the Atlantic, pass through the Mediterranean to the delta of the Nile. Second, you would have to learn hieroglyphics and some pretty funky religious stuff. Third, you would have to dress, eat, work, and commute differently. This, in a nutshell, is the problem of 'hermeneutical distance.' We have these sorts of challenges particularly when we are talking about the

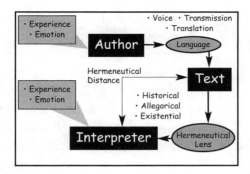

Bible. The words on the page sound familiar to us thanks to years of church traditions, songs, and sermons. But sometimes the familiar sounds are deceptive for we are separated from the text in a number of significant ways. (1) **Time**—we live after Freud, Darwin, the Protestant Reformation, and nuclear bombs; this means we think differently than Peter, Paul, and Mary. (2) **Culture**—in the western world we are democratic capitalists who vote for presidents not peasant Mediterraneans who live under the colonial rule of Roman Emperors. (3) **Language**—Jesus spoke Aramaic, read Hebrew, and was written about in Greek. Most Christians today can't read any of those three languages. (4) **Geography**—so how many camels have you ridden lately? And what does living in a desert region really feel like? Or what about living in a perpetual war zone? (5) **Religion**—Jesus was not a Christian, he was a Jew who wore a prayer shawl, refrained from pork, and worshiped on Saturday. These are all significant barriers, but none are impossible hurdles. Yet, like a track star, if we are to keep from landing on our faces as we run our hurdles, we will need to train a bit to make sure we can rise above our own narrow world and enter into the world(s) of the Bible.

The author wearing a common prayer shawl (Talith) to recreate the Sabbath call on a ram's horn (Shophar).

Summary: Communication is simply the conjunction of an author, a text, and an interpreter. That is simple enough. Yet language is a complicated process because (a) both author and reader have their own experiences and emotions that may hinder proper understanding. Furthermore, (b) all communication is fil-

> *The further the divide between author and interpreter, the greater the effort will have to be to come to within an understanding distance.*

tered through language that is filled with pitfalls one must watch out for. Moreover, (c) what we are looking for (or perhaps how we are looking for it) will determine what we find. Finally, (d) we are separated from the text by time, language, culture, geography, and religion, all of which are difficult hurdles to jump. Add all this up and one might come away with a pretty pessimistic view of understanding anything. Yet the reality is that we *do* understand each other. Mothers tell their children to clean up their rooms and they 'get it' (whether they 'do it' or not is determined by other factors). Women and men actually get married and have families (crossing the male/female divide which is perhaps the most mystifying divide of all human communication). Simply put, language works. Why? Because despite all the difficulties inherent in language, we are somehow able, with courteous listening, to understand one another. Perfectly? No, but we are close enough to buy and sell, make appointments, express our feelings, describe events, and even tell a joke now and then. In short, we can come within *understanding distance* of the author. This point is proved by the very fact you have not yet put down this book as complete nonsense. Communication can work if we work at it.

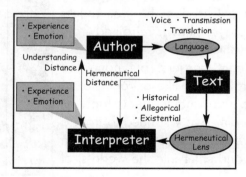

Finishing the Task

The hermeneutical process is not yet finished. Before you can adequately say you comprehend a particular bit of communication, especially from the Bible, you must do two things: Obey and Tell.

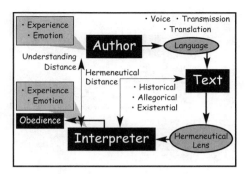

Obedience *is to communication as romance is to a relation-ship.* Flowers and candlelight dinners tell the story of love better than Hallmark cards. Guys, I know this is very odd for you, but women would rather be *shown* your love than told. This is a deliberately chosen metaphor. Jesus said, "If you love me, you will obey what I command" (John 14:15). Is this really much different from a teary-eyed mother who cries to her children, "Why can't you just *listen* to me?" Surely she doesn't mean by 'listen' that your auditory sensory nerves register sound waves! This is a plea for obedience. Parents, lovers, teachers, and coaches all feel the same about this point: "Do what I tell you!" In fact, if you don't obey the words of Scripture, you have no right to claim that you

> *Your hands must heed what your mind concedes.*

understand them. For biblical hermeneutics is about *holistic* understanding. If your feet are not aligned with your cerebellum you cannot claim spiritual comprehension. There is something about the pulsating experience of obedience that enables one to fully grasp the Lord's teaching. It's like the woman (true story) who stood on the precipice overlooking the Oregon coast, soaking in the grandeur of the Pacific for the very first time. After absorbing the sight for a moment she mumbled, ". . . Huh, it's not as big as I thought it would be." Lady, you won't comprehend the vastness of the Pacific until you start to swim! The romance of movies shot at the coast can only be comprehended by those of us who know the suffocating smell of seagulls and seaweed, the flesh-stripping surf, and the angry grip of sand in every orifice after body-surfing. Then, and only then, can you say you understand the ocean. Obedience is not as romantic as you think, but far more invigorating than you imagined.

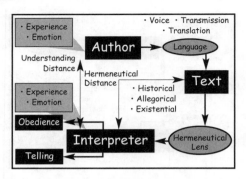

Telling *is to communication what announcement is to an engagement.* Let us return to our patron deity, Hermes. His job was to 'communicate' the message of the Pantheon, not to merely comprehend it. Now, not every Christian is obligated to become a teacher. Yet those who have been privileged with studying the Bible will only find their comprehension complete when they attempt to communicate what they have learned to others. Why? Well, there is something about hearing ourselves say something that powerfully embeds it into our brain. Educators have researched this. The most powerful way of transforming someone's belief system is to have them teach what they have learned. There is another reason: gravitational pull does not exist in an ivory tower—what flies inside the tower may sink like lead in the real world. Lots of ideas sound perfectly good in the privacy of your study, but shrivel more quickly than a truffle when exposed to daylight. Can I make a confession here? Often I have come to the pulpit with a 'brilliant' idea that I was sure would ignite a national revival, only to be rebuked by a corporate bewilderment not dissimilar to what one might expect when seeing a streaker in the

Creativity is never a replacement for clarity.

Vatican. If your ideas fail to impress your audience, it could be due to their 'itching ears'; but a more likely cause is your new-found 'truth' just ain't so. Sometimes we fail hermeneutically because we wanted to sound clever or novel. We must do better than the original Hermes that deceived his hearers; our own pride will have to take a backseat to the needs, wisdom, and practice of the community through which God filters his grand message of salvation.

Three Concluding Clarifications

Before tying a bow around this first chapter, there are three clarifications about hermeneutics that must see the light of day. We mustn't leave you with the wrong impression about the nature of this science and art. First, *sometimes hermeneutics is done consciously but most of the time it is unconscious.* If you have ever learned a foreign language, you know how this works. At first you labor over everything. Vocabulary words are hard and weird. Sentences are put together in a strange order. Figures of speech seem senseless. In fact, at some point you will read a sentence, understand the meaning of every word, but still not know what in the world the author means. It is frustrating. But if you keep at it, one day something magical happens. You read or hear something, and it strikes you that you understood the meaning without translating! You crossed an invisible line and your brain thought in Spanish or French or Arabic. It is truly exhilarating.

> *Newspaper Headline:*
> ## TIGERS MASSACRE INDIANS
> *Depending on the section of the newspaper, you will interpret the message differently, right? The "international news" section describes the death of natives from India, while the "sports" section describes the result of a baseball game between Detroit and Cleveland, and the "local news" section describes an unfortunate incident because of an animal escape at the local zoo near a Native American reservation.*

Likewise, if you have ever traveled out of the country, you know that driving is different, ordering food is different, borders, politics, relationships, etc., etc. are all different. Simply put, when things are foreign to us, we have to make a conscious effort to understand what others are saying and doing. We use artificial props like dictionaries and maps, guidebooks and interpreters. After a while, things get to be more familiar, and we don't have to work so hard. This is what you will experience with the Bible. It is a foreign book about foreign people in foreign places. Give yourself some time to get adjusted to the climate. It will never be as comfortable as reading the newspaper, I suppose, but you will begin to listen better. Why bring this up? Because some say, "We don't need to interpret the Bible, we just read it and obey." WRONG! You interpret all human communication. If you are in your own cultural environment, you do it unconsciously; if you do it in a foreign context, you probably must do it consciously. But whether consciously or unconsciously, language is always interpreted. *And if you try to interpret foreign language with your own native language it won't be long before you make some very serious errors.*

A second clarification, which was alluded to earlier, is that hermeneutics will not solve all your questions about difficult passages. In fact (and I hate to tell you this), by reading this book you are going to have *more* questions than before. Why? Because you will see things you didn't see before. You will learn about textual variants, apparent contradictions, figurative language, problems with application, language barriers, and more. So, be warned. If you prefer a life of simple naïveté, then *put down this book!* If you simply want to "read and obey," even if that requires wearing blinders, then find the nearest exit. Look, there are real problems in understanding the Bible. We simply believe that facing them squarely will put us in a better position to come within understanding distance of the authors. Hermeneutics will not solve all the problems, but it will guide you in the right directions. The bad news is that you will see there are mines out there that must be avoided. The good news is that if you can avoid the land mines there are gold mines beyond.

Third, I want you to know of my own convictions about the Bible. (1) *The Bible is the Word of God.* This carries several important implications. For instance, if it is God's word, then it is understandable. After all, God created humanity, including our linguistic ability. Therefore, he knows how we think and speak. He knows how to say to us what he wants us to know in language that we are able to grasp. (2) *The Bible is inspired.* Honestly, I'm not even sure what all that means. But it has something to do with the Holy Spirit using people to put into words the living message of God. Men like Paul, Luke, and David recorded on scrolls the activities of God in Israel and the Church. It is a story of God's relentless love and miraculous intervention through the person of Jesus. This story is *flawless* in its ability to communicate the message of salvation. It is *truthful* in what it says about God, humanity, evil, ethics, etc. This book is a sufficient guide to every life crisis from raising children to going to war, from your deepest thoughts to your public discourse. And this book is *lovely.* David puts it this way in Psalm 19:7-11:

The law of the LORD is perfect,
    reviving the soul.
The statutes of the LORD are trustworthy,
    making wise the simple.
The precepts of the LORD are right,
    giving joy to the heart.
The commands of the LORD are radiant,
    giving light to the eyes.
The fear of the LORD is pure,
    enduring forever.
The ordinances of the LORD are sure
    and altogether righteous.
They are more precious than gold,
    than much pure gold;
they are sweeter than honey,
    than honey from the comb.
By them is your servant warned;
    in keeping them there is great reward.

Finally, I am convinced that *study of the Bible is the highest form of worship.* Many (read 'most') have substituted the word "music" for "worship." And music is, indeed, an incredibly powerful means of expression. But worship, in its essence, is understanding who God is and who we are in his presence. The Bible, more than the hymnal or chorus chart, is a clear guide to the character of God and the claim he makes over our lives. It is through the Scriptures, more than anything else, that the community of God's people come to understand the revelation of who God is. So come let us worship together.

Going Further:

Assignments and Further Reading

Assignment #1:

✍ Select a text to use throughout the rest of the book as a case study for the tools and principles that you are learning. Remember, meaning is found in pericopes and not in single verses, so choose a section of 6-8 verses and/or a couple of paragraphs (e.g., Col 1:15-23).

✍ Once you have selected your text, write or type out the text inserting a significant amount of space between each line, as shown below:

He is the image of the invisible God, the firstborn over

all creation. For by him all things were created: things

in heaven and on earth, visible and invisible, whether

thrones or powers or rulers or authorities; all things

were created by him and for him.

✍ Read the following short story about looking at a fish: http://www.bethel.edu/~dhoward/resources/Agassizfish/Agassizfish.htm

✍ Next, write out all the observations and questions about your text you can think of (25-30 each). Go crazy here! No question or observation is too trivial or too silly. Ask questions you know cannot be answered; sparking your imagination is as important here as is scientific precision. Here are the kinds of things to look for: literary patterns, repetition, contrasts/comparisons, lists, cause/effect, conclusions, figures of speech, conjunctions, prepositions, pronouns, questions asked. Who wrote this? To whom?

Why? What was going on politically, socially, inside and outside the church? How does this section connect in its literary context? Are there any contradictions or apparent mistakes? If this section of Scripture were not here, what would be missing in the text? How does this text fit into the overall flow and purpose of the book? Why did the author choose this strategy of writing? What is the tone of the passage?

✍ Naturally, your questions and observations will be guided by what text you have chosen to examine. Furthermore, use the above questions as a mere launching board for your own list of questions and observations. These are by no means exhaustive.

Further Reading:

✍ If you don't already have a computer concordance, download your own Bible for easy, computer access to your biblical text at: http://www.bible.org/page.php?page_id=3086 or look at the website appendix for other Bible downloads.

✍ Read this article on Biblical Hermeneutics at: http://hermeneutics.kulikovskyonline.net/hermeneutics/introherm.htm

✍ Search this website to start becoming familiar with various resources online and construct a 'favorites' list on your computer entitled 'Hermeneutics.' Hyperlink five sources from the following website that you find most helpful. http://home.comcast.net/~rciampa/

✍ From the previous website, write down three books you would like to buy to build your Bible study library.

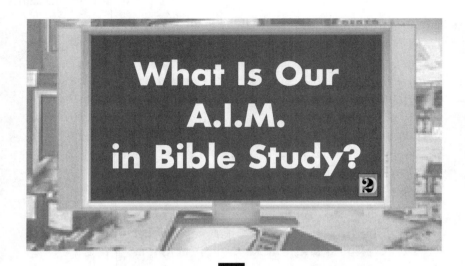

What Is Our A.I.M. in Bible Study?

T he previous chapter answered one simple question: *What is Hermeneutics?* This chapter will address two more questions which will complete our introduction to this study. The two questions both have to do with the purpose of studying the Bible: (1) *Is there only one A.I.M. in the text?* and (2) *Can we find out what is the A.I.M.?* OK, so I suppose you are wondering what this silly little abbreviation 'A.I.M.' stands for. Well, first of all, it is not silly; it is foundational for everything else we will say. In fact, if you don't understand A.I.M., you will be destined to be a hermeneutical midget for the remainder of your natural days. *A.I.M. stands for 'Author's Intended Meaning.'* The A.I.M. *must be* your aim in studying the Bible.

Many Christians gather for Bible studies, read the text, and ask: "What does this text mean to you?" Frankly my dear . . . well, you get the sentiment. It does not matter what the text means to you; what matters is what the author was trying to say. Your *personal* interpretation, opinion, or hypothesis is *almost* completely irrelevant. Can you imagine a physics student reading Einstein's equation, $E=MC^2$, and coming up with a *personal* interpretation? If she writes on the test, "$E=MC^2$ means that **E**veryone **M**atters to **C**hrist Exponentially," not only will she fail the test, she deserves public humiliation even if her answer is theologically sound. Or perhaps you could run a cell phone business and allow each of your customers to *personally* interpret the warranty on the phones you sell. "Of course I took my phone scuba diving with me; right here it says, 'This phone is camera ready,' and I thought I might see some cool fish!" Or perhaps you can picture a traffic cop motioning a car to take a left to avoid a deadly collision. The driv-er waves at the friendly police-man and then turns right any-way, thinking that the hand ges-ture was merely a cordial greet-ing. Well, there's another one for the Darwin Awards!

Every day our lives depend on understanding what other peo-ple are trying to communicate. That's the way traffic signs work; that's the way legal contracts work; and that's the way public edu-cation works. So why do we think we have a right to make the Bible mean what is convenient, comfortable, or culturally accept-able? This is nonsense and it is about time somebody said so. So stand up right now, put your hand over your heart and repeat after me: *"I promise to seek the Author's intended meaning, the whole of the Author's intended meaning, and nothing but the Author's intended meaning, so please help me, God!"*

Seeking the A.I.M. is really quite easy if you have the least bit of imagination. Let me give you this simple little exercise for the next time you are in church, in a Bible study, or even in your per-sonal devotions. After reading the text, picture the author (Paul or Matthew or Jeremiah, etc.) sitting in front of you. Say to them, "This is what you intended this passage to mean. . . ." And, of course, you present to them the interpretation that you just heard or understood. If they look back at you and say, "Huh?" you'll know you're wrong. If, however, they say, "Yep, that's exactly what I meant," then your interpretation is right. Obviously this is an oversimplification, but it works 90% of the time as an effective crap-o-meter. This little exercise will weed out the vast majority of the silliness that inevitably follows the phrase, "This passage means to me. . . ." However, we get ahead of ourselves. First we must ask a critical question.

Is There Really Only One AIM?

Can a passage not mean different things to different people? Please understand, we are not saying that a passage only has one application. Certainly, "love your neighbor" can be applied in a nearly infinite number of ways. When we are talking about the *meaning* of a passage, however, the author really does have one thing in mind. How do we know this?

(1) **God is the source of the Bible**. While we do have a number of human authors, at the end of the day, God guided the writing and collection of each of the sixty-six books. Because God is not schizophrenic, nor does he change, what he says is consistent. Listen to what the Bible says about itself:

> Above all, you must understand that no prophecy of Scripture came about by the prophet's own interpretation. For prophecy never had its origin in the will of man, but men spoke from God as they were carried along by the Holy Spirit. (2 Pet 1:20-21; cf. John 12:49; 1 Cor 14:37; Gal 1:12; 1 Thess 2:13)

If this book called the Bible comes from God, then it is his authoritative word that we listen to on his terms and not on our own. Simply put, treat the Bible like you would the words of your mother. When she tells you to clean your room, it really doesn't matter what *you* think 'clean' is; what matters is *her* definition of 'clean.' If she thinks that clothes strewn from the curtain rods and half-eaten sandwiches under the bed constitute clean, just leave your room in its current evolutionary state of atrophy. If not, you probably need to alter its condition substantially. Your mother has something specific in mind when she uses the word 'clean,' and if you are not out of your mind, you better mind by figuring out what she means by 'clean.'

(2) **The Bible expresses the expectation that we read and understand God's word.** Part of the beauty of the Bible is its simplicity. In fact, God chose *koine* Greek for the New Testament which was the Greek of the common man on the street. This says something about God's desire to speak in understandable ways. Oh sure, there are some difficult passages, particularly because of our historical, linguistic, and cultural distance which

we discussed in the last chapter. However, when most people say, "I just don't understand the Bible," what they really mean is "I'm too lazy to sit down and actually read it carefully." The Bible itself says plainly enough that it is a book which one can read and understand: "For we do not write you anything you cannot read or understand" (2 Cor 1:13). "In reading this, then, you will be able to understand my insight into the mystery of Christ" (Eph 3:4).

> *Literacy rates in the Roman Empire were probably somewhere in the neighborhood of 15%. So most people didn't actually read the Bible themselves, but when it was read publicly, even the simplest of peasants could hear and understand the message. If you would like to practice listening to the Bible, go to* http://www.audiotreasure.com/ *or you can subscribe to "The Bible Podcast" with the* New English Translation *read by Michael Lee.*

(3) **We are told to hold to the traditions**: "What you heard from me, keep as the pattern of sound teaching, with faith and love in Christ Jesus. Guard the good deposit that was entrusted to you—guard it with the help of the Holy Spirit who lives in us" (2 Tim 1:13-14). Now, how can we hold to something inherently unstable or unknowable? If the Bible means many things to many different people, then holding a tradition is as difficult as nailing Jello to a tree. If there is something called 'tradition,' then it must be a specific body of teaching that can be passed down from one generation to the next. Consequently, there is something the biblical authors both inherited and passed on. Thus, there is a stable A.I.M. in the text.

(4) **We are instructed to rebuke deviants** (cf. Matt 15:3-9; Gal 1:6-9; 2 Thess 2:10-12; 1 Tim 4:1-4; 1 Tim 6:3-5; 2 Pet 2:1-3; 2 Pet 3:16-17). How can we do that if there is no "rule"? Gentlemen, you may have experienced this in dating. Just about the time you figure out what your girlfriend wants, she changes her mind. For example, she might complain that you never buy her chocolates. So you buy her chocolates. But you happen to give them to her on one of her 'fat days' when she is feeling bloated and

> *Irrelevant Tangent:*
>
> *Gentlemen, in the course of romance a general rule is that the effectiveness of a romantic gesture, such as chocolates or flowers, is in direct proportion to the number of other women it makes jealous. Thus, your public humiliation generally translates into effective romance (this includes giving her flowers at school and wearing matching sweaters).*

ugly, so you get a tongue lashing. It is very confusing and by every (male) standard quite unfair. Fortunately for most of us romantically challenged males, the Bible is pretty clear about what is expected of us and what is proper doctrine and behavior.

(5) **We are told to have 'one mind'**: "I appeal to you, brothers, in the name of our Lord Jesus Christ, that all of you agree with one another so that there may be no divisions among you and that you may be perfectly united in mind and thought" (1 Cor 1:10; cf. John 17:20-21; Eph 4:1-6; Phil 2:2-5). Now how, pray tell, could we be of one mind if the Scriptures can mean lots of things to different people? That's just nonsense. If we are to agree on something, there must be something upon which to agree. There must be a right doctrine from the single source of God's holy word.

(6) Aside from the passages listed above, **a single A.I.M. is a necessity of human language**. Oh sure, you could have a Hallmark card that means different things to different people. Even a love song can be adopted as 'our song' even if it differs from the author's meaning. But these are poetry, not prose. If real estate contracts could be interpreted 'personally,' life would be chaos. The same could be said for tax laws, marriage vows, college syllabi, and CNN. A single meaning of the author is an obvious and indispensable characteristic of human language. I'm not saying that we 'get it' perfectly or that we need to in order to survive, but as human beings living in social groups, if we can't understand each other, then civilization as we know it is over. If you are still unconvinced, then I challenge you to this simple exercise: Go buy yourself a GPS navigation system and interpret 'personally' the directions of the omniscient lady in the magical little box, and see if you end up where you intended to go.

What It Does NOT Mean to Have a Single A.I.M.

Perhaps some of you are saying, "Wait a minute; are you telling me that *ALL* language has only one meaning?" No, we are saying that *most* language has only one author's intended meaning and that, if you are going to deviate from that, you better have a pretty good reason for doing so. Let me give you four pretty good reasons:

(1) **Some genres are designed to have double meanings.** If you tell a joke or a pun, of course it has two meanings. It was designed *by the author* to have two meanings. This double entendre is what makes it funny! Jokes 'work' when a term is twisted in an unexpected way. Likewise a pun plays off a word's double meaning. In the same way, Jesus' parables are extended metaphors that have both an 'earthly' meaning and a 'heavenly' message by the author's design. Prophecy is another genre that sometimes has double meaning. For example, the virgin of Isaiah 7:14 was a young woman in Isaiah's lifetime that bore a child (in quite the ordinary way) which was a sign of the nation's impending doom. Matthew, however, can use that very same text to show how the birth of Jesus also fulfills this same text in a deeper and more miraculous way when speaking about Jesus' virginal conception. So obviously, some genres are *designed* to have double meanings just as some prophecies can have multiple fulfillments.

> ### JOKES!
>
> **#1: What is it like to you?**
> Mortal: *What is a million years like to you?*
> God: *Like one second.*
> Mortal: *What is a million dollars like to you?*
> God: *Like one penny.*
> Mortal: *Can I have a penny?*
> God: *Just a second.*
>
> **#2: Questions for Thought**
> Q: *Who was the greatest female financier in the Bible?*
> A: *Pharaoh's daughter. She went down to the bank of the Nile and drew out a prophet.*
>
> Q: *What do they call pastors in Germany?*
> A: *German Shepherds.*
>
> Q: *What kind of man was Boaz before he got married?*
> A: *Ruth-less.*
>
> Source: Aha! Jokes,
> http://www.AhaJokes.com//religious_jokes.html

(2) Meaning is singular, interpretations multiple, and applications infinite. When an author speaks, writes, or acts, he means something specific by that communication. S/he intends to communicate a particular message to a specific audience. Thus, **meaning** is singular. However, we are not always able to get at the author's intended meaning. Some passages are tricky because the author has not been clear, because the background is illusive, or because the historical details or translations are sketchy. So when we encounter these difficult texts, we make educated guesses based on the meaning of words, the literary structure of the passage, the context, genre, parallel passages, and cultural setting. Based on these facts, we can suggest several possible **interpretations** of 'problem passages' and commend the most likely meaning of the author based on the exegetical possibilities. Finally, when it comes time to apply the text to a modern audience, there could be dozens of appropriate **applications** in various life situations and cultural settings.

(3) **There are *inferences* based on the author's meaning that may be necessary but should not be treated as inspired**. For example, Paul said that an elder should be the husband of one wife and rule his family well. Does that mean a man cannot be an elder if he is single or if he has had no children? Is that a *necessary* inference based on this text? Does Paul's participation in the Lord's Supper on the first day of the week (Acts 20:7) necessarily imply that a weekly celebration of the Lord 's Supper is a precedent for us to follow? Peter said, "Repent and be baptized in the name of Jesus Christ." Does that mean that baptism should always happen at conversion rather than sometime later in a person's spiritual journey?

> ***Example:***
> *What did Jesus mean when he changed Simon's name to Peter (=Petros) and promised to build his church on this 'rock' (=petra)? The Catholic interpretation is that Peter himself is the rock, i.e., the first Pope, and the church is founded on his leadership. The common Protestant interpretation is that Peter is a petros (small rock), but his confession is a boulder (petra) large enough for the church to stand upon. An ecumenical possibility is that Peter is representative of the Twelve and that their combined leadership is the foundation of the church (cf. Eph 2:20). All three are potential interpretations of Jesus' meaning.*
>
> ***Hint:***
> *If you read a commentary and they offer more than five possible meanings of a text, they are probably just guessing!*

Such implications are always additions to the meaning of the text and are often dangerous because they can easily import someone's theological or cultural bias. For example, I have often heard teachers justify a ban on smoking because our body is the temple of the Holy Spirit (1 Cor 6:19). This is problematic at two levels. First, why is smoking or drinking the sin singled out rather than overeating, caffeine, sugar, preservatives, lack of exercise, workaholism, or environmental issues such as air-pollution, chemical preservatives, pesticides, or carcinogens? Are not each of these also destructive to the human body? Second, and more exegetically profound, is the fact that when the Bible speaks of the 'body' being indwelt by the Holy Spirit, the primary issue is the Church being the temple of the Holy Spirit, not the individual Christian. All the verses that speak of the Holy Spirit in the body have the *church* primarily in view, not the *individual* (cf. 1 Cor 3:16; 6:19 [cf. v. 15]; Eph 2:22; 1 John 4:13). Our confusion comes from reading these passages with an individualistic Western mind-set rather than an Eastern, group-oriented worldview. In summary, one must be careful to distinguish between the plain meaning of Scripture and the implications (some quite valid) that are drawn from that meaning.

(4) **Ambiguity is a valid and important literary device**. Just because a text is confusing does not mean that it is a poor literary piece. If you have ever come in late from a date and your parents asked you, "What kept you so late?" then you realize that ambiguity can be your friend. Politicians, lawyers, and used car salesmen often use ambiguity to their professional advantage. Ambiguity, however, is not only a tool of disingenuous communicators; it is also a tool of good educators. Jesus' parables were deliberately designed to make people think long and hard about the meaning of the 'simple' story. Prophets often used ambiguity to force reflection about the nation's behavior and destiny. What I'm saying is this: Ambiguity may make a text look confusing, like there is no clear A.I.M., but sometimes the aim is not clear meaning but deep reflection. At that point, ambiguity is just the right literary device to accomplish the task of the text.

Summary: There is only one A.I.M. in most passages. Authors speak and write so that their meaning will be clearly understood. However, there are certain literary devices (parables, puns, jokes, and ambiguity) that purposefully employ multiple meanings. Moreover, sometimes texts are too far distanced from us so that the clear meaning has been lost. At that point we make educated guesses (interpretations) about what is the most likely meaning. In addition, any given text might have multiple inferences and applications, but these are not the same as multiple meanings. Bottom line: most of the time there is only one A.I.M. Therefore, if you are going to suggest multiple meanings for a particular text, you better have a pretty good reason for doing so. This leads to a second question.

Can We Get the A.I.M.?

It is one thing to affirm that there is a single meaning for most Bible passages. It is quite another thing to assert that we are capable of retrieving that A.I.M. After all, there are two *significant* obstacles in the way: Hermeneutical Distance and Preunderstanding. Let's deal with each in turn.

Hermeneutical Distance

In the previous chapter we defined hermeneutical distance as those things which stand between you and the text: time, language, culture, geography, and religion. We pointed out just how difficult it can be to go back into the biblical world to feel what they felt, to see what they saw, and to hear what they heard. There are substantial challenges in thinking like a first-century Mediterranean Jew! What makes matters worse is that language is innately slippery and given to multiple potential meanings. Moreover, interpreters are fallible, finite, and biased. So we have a distant text, in slippery language, read by imperfect interpreters. What a combination! Don't pack your bags just yet. While the challenges are weighty and real, so are our tools and advantages.

(1) **God spoke to people in language that he created.** God knows how our brains work, and he used natural human language to communicate the ideas necessary for us to have a relationship with him. In short: God spoke on our terms and he is pretty good at it. If you believe that God created the world (a pretty good bet), that he loved the world he created (a pretty good bet), and that he desired to communicate that love to us (another pretty good bet), then the question of competence is not primarily on the human side but on the side of the divine. Could God create the human mind with the ability to understand the divine message? I'm gonna say 'yes'! Furthermore, human language works every day and has since the days of prehistoric humanity. The fact that human beings live in communities, send text messages, listen to the radio, tell stories, and write books is fairly convincing evidence that this human ability of language functions substantially well.

(2) We were created in the image of God (Gen 1:26) and our minds were renewed by the Holy Spirit (1 Cor 2:16). The human ear is a wonderfully complex creation. It starts with a conclave elastic cartilage specifically designed to funnel sound waves to the tympanic membrane which translates

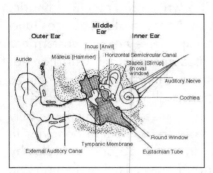

these waves to three miniature bones which sense the minutest vibration. These bones, in turn, reflect the reverberation through a circular chamber filled with fluid and tiny hair-like nerves which translate nearly infinite combinations of sounds to the auditory nerve. It is truly extraordinary! The tangible evidence of God's good creation is as plain as the nose on your face (or in this case, the ears on your head). Does it not stand to reason, therefore, that God gave equally excellent mental faculties to understand language? Why would he give us ears to hear but not a mind to understand? Furthermore, if God gave us such good physical and mental apparatuses with which to enjoy sound and understanding, would he not also give us the spiritual capacity to add wisdom to our hearing?

Just as a musician can train his ears and a student can train his mind, the Christian can also train his spiritual perception. How? It comes through obedience. Jesus said, "If anyone chooses to do God's will, he will find out whether my teaching comes from God or whether I speak on my own" (John 7:17). Again, in John 8:31-32, he said, "If you hold to my teaching, you are really my disciples. Then you will know the truth, and the truth will set you free." Our spiritual perception is directly tied to our practice of Jesus' commands. So if you want to understand the Bible better, do what it says. Some people don't understand the Bible because they are not willing to put into practice the little they do understand. The Bible is more like auto mechanics than philosophy. In order to understand philosophy you need to wrap your mind around deep thoughts. In order to understand auto mechanics you need to wrap your hand around a wrench. That's certainly not to argue that Christianity has no deep thoughts. Theology is obviously a mind-blowing endeavor. Yet it is most often in the *practice* of Christian principles that a person's perception is expanded and certain Bible passages are comprehended.

(3) Hermeneutical principles are universal. The principles outlined in this book could be written in French, Amharic, or Cuneiform — it really doesn't matter because all languages function by these same rules. These principles are neither western nor eastern, modern nor ancient, educated nor ignorant, Christian nor pagan. They are human. God built these hermeneutical principles into the universe and they are as universal as the human need for oxygen, love, and significance. In this sense, hermeneutics is truly scientific because it is based upon observing human behavior in native environments and extracting from that observation rules by which language operates. The good news is that though the process is complex, it is also innate. Therefore, we are not teaching you anything you don't already know, we are simply helping you use common sense to wisely apply the principles you have practiced since you were two.

Hermeneutical Virtues:

Just as in kindergarten your teacher called on you to practice "fair play" that you already instinctively knew was right, so now, we are calling you to hermeneutical "fair play" in order to effectively listen to the word of God. These seven hermeneutical virtues must guide your study of the Bible:

1. **Listen courteously**. Listen to your dialogue partner from his/her perspective without trying to force them to say what you think they should be saying. If you repeat back to them what they just said in your own words, they should nod and say, "Yep, you got it!"
2. **Listen attentively**. Real listening is hard work. Pay attention to the details, the context, the purpose of what they are saying, the emotional tone, and what they are trying to accomplish through their communication.
3. **Listen generously**. If you love the person you are listening to, you will hear his heart, not just his words, and you will tend to give him the benefit of the doubt when something is unclear or apparently inaccurate. Do that with the Bible.

---

4. **Listen humbly**. We listen to mentors we respect differently than we listen to our little brother because we assume our mentors have something valuable to teach us. Take that posture of humility with everyone you listen to (especially biblical authors) and you will learn much.

5. **Listen practically**. Listen as if you were reading a recipe from a cook book or a manual for your new computer. You are going to implement this stuff so look for practical applications.

6. **Listen artistically**. Every communicative act comes packaged in some genre and form. Pay attention to the artistic presentation, not merely the content of the communication.

7. **Listen communally**. The Bible was written to the church, not to individuals. So even if you are studying alone, you should always hear the voices of notable teachers both past and present whether it is through books, CDs, websites, or pod casts.

(4) There are tons of hermeneutical helps. Sure we are separated from the author by geography, language, and culture, but if National Geographic can take you to the world's most exotic places and if the History Channel can take you back in time, why can't Bible scholars provide resources that do the same thing? That fact is they can, they have, and they do. For example, if you don't speak Greek or Hebrew, you will be dependent on a good **translation** of the Bible. If you have never traveled to the Middle East, you will want to pick up a good **Bible Atlas** that includes lots of pictures. Or better yet, just go online to one of the free sites that provide study helps for geography, topography, flora and fauna of the region as it pertains to each text you are studying.[1]

> ### *Popular Bible Versions*
>
> **The New International Version (NIV)** – *This translation of the Bible was completed by a panel of the best biblical translators of our recent time. The goal was to translate the biblical text close to the original languages from the most dependable manuscripts, but in a manner that was reader-friendly for today.*
>
> **The New King James Version (NKJV)** – *This translation of the Bible is a more updated version of the KJV, in that it still uses the poetic language from the 1611 version but in a more updated vernacular.*

[1] Try http://www.biblemap.org/ or http://www.bible-history.com/maps/.

The New Revised Standard Version (NRSV) – *This translation developed from a committee created from the National Council of Churches. This version intentionally avoided the use of "thee" and "thou" that the RSV included, and also attempts to have a more gender inclusive tendency.*

The New American Standard Bible (NASB) – *The NASB prides itself on being the most literally translated from the original languages of the available English versions. The translators intentionally tried to avoid interpretative translation where possible.*

The Message Bible – *Eugene Peterson, the translator of The Message, specifically translated The Message Bible as an interpretative paraphrase for the common person in the pew. As a local pastor, he found that when he translated books of the Bible for his congregation in their everyday language, the passages would blossom for them. This experience led to the translation of the entire Bible in common, everyday language of today.*

Perhaps there are some biblical terms, people, and places that are unfamiliar to you. Here you can find help through a good **Bible Dictionary** whether it is in print [2] or free online.[3] **Archaeologists** have found thousands of items that help illustrate and/or confirm the biblical text.[4] This is an area well worth investigating. In addition to archaeology, one should investigate the **sociology** of the ancient world to discover how people lived everyday life.[5] These scholars will help you get a feel for how life worked in that world and what the text means against the backdrop of ancient social customs. *In short, there is no excuse for not crossing the bridge between the modern and ancient world.* We have all the tools necessary to understand (not perfectly but thoroughly) the cultural, historical, geographical, literary, and linguistic world of the Bible.

[2] Check out these dictionaries: Walter A. Elwell, *Baker Theological Dictionary of the Bible* (Grand Rapids: Baker Academic, 2001); J.D. Douglas and Merrill C. Tenney, *Zondervan's Pictorial Bible Dictionary* (Grand Rapids: Zondervan, 1999); and Craig A. Evans and Stanley Porter, eds., *Dictionary of New Testament Background* (Downers Grove, IL: InterVarsity, 2000).

[3] Try http://eastonsbibledictionary.com/ or http://www.bible-history.com/smiths/

[4] Check out http://www.biblicalarcheology.net/ and http://www.biblicalarchaeology.org/.

[5] Look at http://www.middletownbiblechurch.org/biblecus/biblec.htm or http://www.crivoice.org/historyculture.html.

Preunderstanding

A second barrier which keeps us from getting the A.I.M. is our preunderstanding. This is a psychological barrier. Our brains can only take in so much information, so they always try to make sense out of the data we receive. Our brains use two mental tools to help this process: assimilation and gestalt.

> Preunderstanding: *your assumptions and prejudices about how life works.*

Assimilation is the process whereby new data is connected to or incorporated with information we have already understood and organized in our brains. For example, if you see a new animal at the zoo, your brain automatically compares it to other animals you have seen. Thus you intuitively categorize this new animal as a reptile, bird, spider, or mammal. For example, when the

The Duck-Billed Platypus: Fact or Fiction?

duck-billed platypus was first discovered in the western world in the late 1700s, there was great skepticism about it. The first examiners were British scientists who were initially convinced that an Asian taxidermist had sewn the bill of a duck onto the body of a mammal. It didn't fit any known category, thus many people labeled it a hoax.

The second mental tool is **gestalt**. It is the process whereby an image is completed by the brain because the brain always attempts a logical organization of data. You can see half of a picture or an incomplete painting and your brain automatically fills in the details. Try out this audio gestalt exercise: Ask a friend, "What do you call it when someone tells you something funny?" Well, that's a 'joke'. OK,

Circles and the Mind

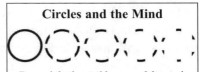

Even while the visible area of the circle diminishes, the mind fills in the gaps so that when there is more missing than visible we can still recognize it as a circle

what is that thing that farmers used to put on the shoulders of oxen when they plowed a field? That's a 'yoke'. OK, what do you call the white of an egg? They will likely answer, 'yolk.' But the correct answer is 'the white of an egg.' You see, our minds try to categorize data according to familiar patterns regardless if it is correct or not.

OK, so what does all this have to do with interpreting the Bible? When we read the Bible, our brains naturally attempt to assemble the data into known categories and fill in the gaps of incomplete data to paint a picture that is comprehensible to our previous knowledge base. For example, when we think about women's roles, we subconsciously attempt to fit the biblical text into categories and experiences of 21st-century women. Or when we read about families, we automatically picture modern, Western, nuclear families. When we encounter a wedding in the Bible our brains conjure up images of white dresses, churches, flower girls, and tuxedos. Obviously, we are trying to make sense of what we are reading by picturing it with our known categories. That is natural, and sometimes helpful, but the obvious danger is painting a picture that is familiar to us but that would be foreign to the biblical author.

These preunderstandings surface at so many levels. There are *cultural* preunderstandings of things like farming, economics, politics, funerals, war, and pets. There are *psychosocial* preunderstandings concerning individualism, freewill, separation of church and state, unlimited supply of honor, environmentalism, etc. There are *historical* presuppositions such as 9/11, the nuclear bomb, and Hitler, all of which shape our views on politics, religion, media, and social values. Individuals can also have their values shaped by the kind of education they receive, the job they perform, their gender, the number of siblings they have, whether their parents were divorced, a crippling disease, where they were raised, etc. What I'm saying is that our life experiences constantly shape and often determine our thinking about new data we receive, and this includes our reading of the Bible.

So, *are we imprisoned by our preunderstandings and destined to read the Bible in certain ways?* If that were true, we would all be destined to remain in our current state of ignorance and narrow understandings. Fortunately, God has provided for us psychological and intellectual tools to ensure our continued growth.

One of the tools we have is *shared similar emotional experiences.* Part of belonging to humanity means experiencing pain, joy, longing, frustration, love, etc. This thought struck me with particular force a number of years ago in a museum in Athens. I was looking at tombstones from about two hundred years before Christ and one caught my eye. A little girl about seven years old had died and her parents had a picture of her carved into her tombstone. In the picture was a little bird in a cage that was obviously her pet. She had a doll in her hand (which she had undoubtedly named) and a little puppy was jumping up on her, licking her hand. I began to weep because I had a little girl about her same age and I suddenly shared that couple's sorrow over the loss of their beloved child more than two thousand years ago. Because of our capacity for both sympathy and empathy we can break through our previous preunderstandings to a new level of awareness. Of course major life changes can cause us instantly to rework our pre-understandings. The death of a spouse, a crippling illness, or a new birth will instantly change the way we perceive reality, including our reading of the Bible. Perhaps you have found yourself reading the Bible with new intensity and interest after a crisis that forces you to rework your presuppositions or prejudices.

Not only can we share life experiences and universal emotions, we share *spiritual longings* to know God, to understand the afterlife, to deal with guilt, and find significance. Hence, when the Bible describes heaven or hell, when Jesus teaches on prayer, when Paul talks about the work of the Holy Spirit, these words tap into a universal spiritual longing that resonates with us. It is kind of like a domesticated wolf that hears his wild cousin call in the distance. There is some instinctual longing within the animal. Likewise, we humans have an instinct to know God. We have a shared sense of eternity in our hearts.

Furthermore, we, as human beings, share certain intellectual capacities such as language, logic, intuition, and imagination. No culture or historical period has a monopoly on these intellectual capacities. These are gifts from God that enable us to put ourselves in other people's shoes. As a result, we have this human capacity of empathy. We can bridge the gap between our own life and the life of the 'other.' Because of this capacity, presuppositions are not prisons, but platforms. They provide for us a place to stand without nailing our feet to the floor.

There is no question that preunderstanding is hard to change. It is resilient, and should be, for this is the grounding that gives us cognitive equilibrium. But the fact is, you are not the same person you were three years ago, and obviously in another ten you will be very different than you are now. This is all the proof we need that our preunderstandings change, providing us with ever-changing and often increasing insights into the biblical text.

Conclusion

Our aim in Bible study is the A.I.M. Yes, there is just one A.I.M. and yes, we have the tools to comprehend it. Perfectly? Of course not. The point, however, is not perfection, but proximity. We are attempting to come close enough to the author that we can listen respectfully, even virtuously to what the other person is saying. No doubt, there are some obstacles (every couple knows that!). But these obstacles of hermeneutical distance and preunderstanding can be overcome if we want badly enough to hear what the Bible is saying and are willing to make the effort to listen attentively.

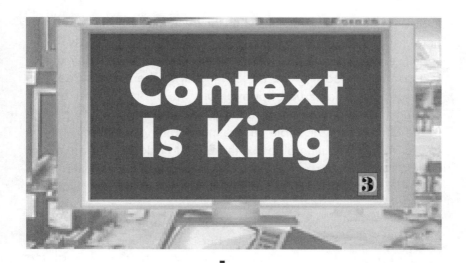

Context Is King

3

If you are to be a *bona fide* Bible student, you **must** learn this mantra. Repeat after me: Context is King, context is King, context is King. In terms of biblical interpretation there is nothing more important for understanding the Scriptures than context. We make more errors by jerking passages out of context than all other kinds of errors combined! You simply **must** respect the context of Scriptures.

So first of all, let's be clear about what we mean by context. We will eventually discuss three levels of context: *cultural context, historical context,* and *literary context.* Just so we can get the lay of the land, let's briefly summarize each of those three kinds of contexts.

First, by **cultural context** we mean *your own life situation.* As we discussed in the first chapter, every Bible reader comes to the text with his or her own life experience. That is your cultural context. In some ways that will keep you from reading the Bible accurately. For instance, single people really can't relate so well to the Song of Songs (or at least one would hope). So the medieval monks, for whom this book was a favorite, *allegorized* the text and read into it

> *Allegorize:* to interpret the text as a symbol of deeper spiritual meaning rather than the obvious historic or literal reality. This method was developed by Origen (185–254 C.E.). Sometimes this is appropriate but more often it is sorely abused. Two examples of allegory in devotional material that have been a great blessing to the church include: Pilgrim's Progress *by Paul Bunyan and* The Chronicles of Narnia *by C.S. Lewis.*

their own mystic relationship with Jesus. While this may be beneficial for singles, it is not likely what Solomon intended given his, shall we say, *active* love life. Another way our own cultural context can make reading the Bible difficult is when we are dealing with specific social issues. For example, the abortion issue, human cloning, and democracy are deeply held values for many people in the church. But the Bible says almost nothing concerning these issues. When we attempt to use the Bible to address certain social issues, we find ourselves tempted toward *eisegesis* rather than *exegesis*. On the other hand, some social issues like women's roles, homosexuality, or divorce are hard

> **Exegesis:** *drawing meaning out of the text.*
> **Eisegesis:** *importing meaning into the text.*

to teach accurately, *not* because the Bible *isn't* clear but because social pressure to say the 'politically correct' thing is all too clear. Often this tempts us to read the Bible in ways that are convenient (or at least more accepted) rather than listening to the author respectfully. Cultural context is a critical concern. We must learn how to bring the ancient text into the modern world with respect and integrity for both. This discussion will be fleshed out when we talk about application of Scripture. For now, we will leave cultural context off to the side and concentrate on a different kind of context.

Historical Context is the second kind of context. It is similar to modern cultural context, only this pertains to life 2,000 years ago. Instead of asking, "How does this strike *us*?" we ask, "How did this strike *them*?" We need to ask what stuff meant to the original audience of the biblical books. What were the headlines of the local news? Who were the contemporary politicians? How did one go about getting a wife? What did they eat and where did they sleep? What did the music in the temple sound like? How many people got battered by police or cheated in business? These questions are both fascinating and endless. Some of them have concrete answers, others are just good guesses, still others have vanished completely in the mist of time. If we make no attempt, however, to answer these questions, we are free to deceive ourselves into thinking that Jesus was a middle-class American Democrat (or whatever other

> *The Bible cannot mean today what it could not have meant when it was originally written.*

image you happen to see in the mirror). The rule here is that we must know what the Bible meant to the people of its own day before we can appropriately apply it to the people of our day. Frankly, this is one of the most fruitful, interesting, and rewarding areas of biblical studies because of the wealth of information we have in archaeology, history, and cultural studies. However, this too is a subject for a future chapter. Very shortly we will devote an entire portion of this study to the investigation of historical backgrounds but for now we must bid farewell, until we meet again.

What we intend to talk about here is **literary context.** Simply put, this is the text that immediately surrounds a passage. Biblical authors don't just dump a trunk of junk onto the page and let you arrange it how you see fit. Each verse is part of a bigger statement (paragraph). And each of these statements is part of a larger argument (chapter). And these arguments are strung together to develop a thesis (book). The

> **Context:** *This word is derived from two Latin words: con, meaning with and textus, meaning woven cloth. Hence the context implies the connections of the parts to the whole.*

goal of the Bible student is to see how these various parts fit together. It is not so much like puzzle pieces (though that is not an altogether poor metaphor), rather it is more like gears of a clock. Each one drives another so that the whole is greater than the sum of its parts. One must see the whole before the parts make sense. Or perhaps you could think of it as a river that comes from upstream and flows down to the next little village. With any given verse there is always an upstream which you need to know before you drink the water. And with any given verse there is always a downstream so that what happens on the banks where you stand will affect what happens below (just ask the citizens of Las Vegas if they care what happens to the Colorado River!). We must always trace the flow of an argument through the entire book to fully appreciate what is happening in any given spot. To that end, *the goal of this chapter is to learn how to identify the context of any given verse of the Bible and to interpret that verse in the flow of the larger argument.*

Warning! Caution! ¡Cuidado!

Before we move on to talk about *how* to recognize literary context, we want to warn you *what* will keep you from finding it. There are at least four things. First, *memorizing Bible verses* can cloud cogent cognition concerning context (my apologies, I was just entertaining myself). Yes, that's right. Memorizing individual Bible verses has been one of the worst practices for correct understanding of the Bible. Don't get me wrong, Bible memorization is a wonderful thing. In fact, I would argue that it is the single most important exercise for correct understanding of the Bible. The problem comes when we isolate a *single* verse, commit it to memory, but have no idea where it comes from, why it was said, or how it functions in the overall argument.

Let me give you two of the very worst examples. Philippians 4:13 says, "I can do everything through him who gives me strength." This verse is used to make the average Christian into a

superhero. I was working out at a gym a few years ago during a youth conference. A couple of freshmen came in and tried their hand at the bench press. They lay down on the bench and put two 45 pound weights on the bar, totaling 135 pounds including the weight of the bar. The dull thud on the boy's sternum was a sign that perhaps he had attempted too much. As our little wannabe body-builder groaned and wheezed the bar back up, his friend exhorted him, "You can do it! You can do it!" (spouted with all the testosterone of a pubescent teen). Then he said it . . . and I couldn't believe my ears . . . "You can do all things, All Things, ALL THINGS through Christ who gives you strength!" In his defense, he did get the bar up (once). But if Christ strengthens us, then why not load up a couple hundred pounds more?! I've heard this verse quoted for overcoming a bad breakup, getting into a college, and even a young girl with Muscular Dystrophy claimed this promise, not for herself, but for the motorized wheelchair which she (unsuccessfully) attempted to get across a deep ditch. Perhaps instead of claiming miraculous powers for her chair she should have just attempted to rise and walk herself. You might think me cruel for saying this, but I think what is truly cruel is making false promises that God never intended so that we wind up disillusioning well-meaning Christians. Listen, if we make promises through verses jerked from context, they cease to have God's authoritative power. What Paul was talking about was *his own* ability, not yours. Philippians 4:13 is not a promise; it is a personal claim of the Apostle. Furthermore, it is in the context of living with contentment whether rich or poor; go ahead, read the context and see if I'm lying. Perhaps a better application of Philippians 4:13 would be one's willingness to live in poverty for the sake of spreading the Gospel *rather than* getting a high-paying job by the 'power of Christ.'

Another verse that is frequently misquoted is Matthew 18:20, "For where two or three come together in my name, there am I with them." You will hear this most often when people discuss a worship service or youth group meeting, especially one that is poorly attend-

ed. "Well, not many people showed up tonight, but you know what the Bible says, 'Where two or three are gathered. . . .'" Jesus is *not* saying that he will meet us for worship even if very few show up! He was there before anyone showed up and stayed long after! Our gathering does not somehow magically invoke his presence. The context of this pas-

"I wish someone else would show up so Jesus could come in with me!"

sage is about disciplining an erring brother. Specifically, if two or three brothers come to a decision that another is in sin, they have Jesus' legal authority to carry out discipline on him, even leading to excommunication. The Jewish background of this action, of course, is the Mosaic legislation that called for two-three witnesses to carry out a death sentence (to which excommunication is essentially equivalent). Rather than justifying small worship services, this text is a legal ordinance for carrying out one of the most *neglected* practices of the modern western church—discipline of wayward members. Whew, ok, now that I have that off my chest we can move on.

A second bad practice for context is *using single verses as amulets*. We have 'power verses' pinned to our mirror or bumper-sticker; they are plastered on our church marquis and our witness-wear logos; they find their way to plaques on artwork and banners for revivals. We thus have power to "Mount up with Eagle's Wings," "Walk through the valley of the shadow of death," or "leap tall buildings in a single bound." We seem to feel that the very citation of a passage will ward off demons, liberals, vegetarians, and other icky things. This, in fact, is a very old practice. The Jews used to (some still do) wear what were called phylacteries. They were little boxes strapped to the forehead and the left arm and they contained miniature scrolls of Scriptures (usually Deut. 6:4-6). Why? Because Deuteronomy 6 says to teach the Scriptures to your children and in verse 8 we read, "Tie them as symbols on your hands and bind them on your foreheads." The Jewish Rabbis took this literally. Then they started competing with each other for the size of their boxes because the bigger the box the more room for Scripture, the more room for Scripture, the more obviously spiritual you were. For this very practice Jesus offered a scathing rebuke (Matt 23:5). Is this any different from what we do as Christians? The power of the Bible is in knowing the message of God embedded in the text. There is no more magical power in the written words than in the water of baptism, the emblems of communion, or the church building. Inscribing texts may be good for ecclesiastical art but it has virtually no power to make you a better person or even a better student of the word.

A worshiper at the Wailing Wall with a phylactery on his head

A third practice that has hindered our attention to context is *concordance work*. Do you know what a concordance is? These little beauties are incredible gifts for Bible study. A concordance is a book (or a computer program) that lists every word in the Bible and where it is found. Can I make a confession to you? I

For a free online concordance try:
http://www.blueletterbible.org/index.html

love concordances so much that I own ten different kinds. Most are in English but I also have a number which are either in Greek or Hebrew. These tools are indispensable for doing word studies. The problem, however, is when you read fifty, one hundred, or even five hundred uses of a word or phrase in individual verses. Who really takes the time to read each passage in context? I don't want to downplay the occasional need to look at every use of a word or phrase, but if you are going to use any particular verse authoritatively, you simply must read it in context.

You cannot assume that reading a single verse will capture its meaning. It must be read in context. Did you know that the very verse numbers, so helpful in Bible drills, are artificial? They were not added until the 13th

Meaning resides not in words, or even sentences, but in paragraphs.

century and, in fact, many of them are very poorly placed! You simply cannot trust that verse numbers or even chapter divisions will give you the proper context for your verse. [For example, Acts 8:1a really belongs with 7:60!] *In fact, in order to do proper Bible study you must stop thinking verses and start thinking paragraphs.* Only then will you be adequately postured to hear what the author intended to say. Are you ready now to learn *how* to identify the context of a verse? If your answer is "NO," then I will cordially leave you with these three verses, quoted out of context: "Judas went out and hanged himself; go thou and do likewise, and what you do, do quickly," (Matt 27:5b; Luke 9:60; Luke 3:11; John 13:27b).

How to Identify the Parameters of Context

What we're asking here is this: How can we know where one **pericope** ends and another one begins? In other words, para-

Pericope: *A 'chunk' of text with independent meaning. It is roughly equivalent to a 'paragraph.'*

graphs have to be indented somewhere. Who figures that out and how? Well, the *who* is simple—the translators or editors of a Bible version. As a general rule, they get it right. However, you should know that while the texts are inspired, their translations are not. That includes not only their wording but also their editing. Sometimes it's just badly misleading. For example, everyone has heard that the Bible teaches women to be in submission to men. That's true. Take a peek at Ephesians 5:22, "Wives, submit to your husbands as to the Lord." Unfortunately, there is a major paragraph division, including an editor's section title between verses 22 and 21. However, verse 21 says, "Submit to one another out of reverence for Christ." Do you suppose our reading of wives submitting to their husbands should be considered in the light of the fact that all of us submit to one another out of reverence for Christ? In other words, while women should submit to their husbands, they are not the only ones who should be submissive. This illustrates why you need to figure out for yourself where the pericope you're studying begins and ends.

> *Other examples of poor divisions would include: Acts 8:1; Isa 53:1; 2 Cor 2:1.*

OK, so now the *how*: Change or repetition. If something in the text changes suddenly, that is a pretty good indication that the context is taking a turn. This is often marked by transitional prepositions such as 'therefore,' 'thus,' 'however,' 'but,' 'now,' etc. Other structural changes are possible as well. For instance, a verb tense could go from past to present; the sentence could move from first person ("I/we") to third person ("it/she/they"); or the scene could change from one location to another. Any of these kinds of changes could mark a new context. Furthermore, repetition might mark a new cycle in the text. For example, the book of Hebrews has a string of exhortations: "Let us . . ." (4:1,11; 6:1; 10:35-36; 12:1; 13:15). These mark significant sections of the book. Likewise, Malachi is marked by a series of rhetorical questions (1:2,6,7; 2:14,17; 3:8,13), and Micah commands the peoples of the earth (1:2), the Heads of Jacob (3:1), and the mountains (6:1) to "hear the word of the Lord." These rhetorical repetitions function like the chorus of a song that not only repeats a theme but indicates to the listener that a new verse is on its way. Writers want their readers to be able to follow their train of thought, so they will intentionally imbed these kinds of markers into the text. The following section will unpack how this often works.

The Structure of the Book

Once you've marked off the boundaries of the pericope, you need to see how it functions in the overall structure of the book. Your text, you see, is like a brick which fits together with other bricks in the overall pattern and structure of a building. Thus, authors are like artistic masons who not only 'construct concepts' but do so with aesthetically interesting patterns. They 'lay their bricks' so as to create a design that catches the eye. This is true for every book of the Bible except: Psalms, Proverbs, and James. The collection of Psalms is not arranged in any particular order. Thus, each poem/song pretty much stands on its own. The same is true for the collection of Proverbs in which the only real context is a few categories of sayings that are clustered under their topical headings such as 'Adultery' (chs. 5 & 7), 'Wisdom' (ch. 8), and 'The Model Wife' (ch. 31). Last but not least, the book of James is like a phone conversation with your Dad after you've gone off to college: it is a miscellany of advice that may or may not be cogently connected. He's just telling you everything you need to know as it comes to his mind. So there you have the only three books of the Bible where context is of little consequence. In every other biblical book, their authors take great pains to orchestrate their 'bricks' into a beautiful masterpiece. They come in a variety of patterns:[1]

Chronological: Genesis, Exodus, Joshua, 1 & 2 Kings, 1 & 2 Chronicles
Biographical: Ruth, 1 & 2 Samuel, Esther, Matthew, Mark, Luke, John
Geographical: Nehemiah, Jonah, Acts
Cyclical: Judges, Job, Ecclesiastes, Song of Songs, Revelation
Logical: Romans, Galatians, Ephesians, Philippians, Colossians, Hebrews

[1]These labels are both artificial and inconsistent. That is, one could articulate the categories with a number of different labels and some of the books share qualities of more than one category. Nonetheless, these labels help put into perspective the literary artistry used to construct the books of the Bible.

Topical:	Leviticus, Numbers, Deuteronomy, Ezra, Lamentations, 1 & 2 Corinthians, 1 & 2 Thessalonians, 1 & 2 Timothy, Titus, Philemon, 1 & 2 Peter, 1–3 John, Jude
Visionary:	Isaiah, Jeremiah, Ezekiel, Daniel, Hosea, Joel, Amos, Obadiah, Micah, Nahum, Habakkuk, Zephaniah, Haggai, Zechariah, Malachi

Let's take a look at just a few of these to see how complex they can be. **Matthew** is the story of Jesus' life and death. But did you know he arranges his material around five major sermons (chapters 5–7; 10; 13; 18; 24)? Each sermon ends with a choral refrain: "When Jesus had finished saying these things. . . ." Hence, Matthew has deliberately marked off these five sermons and arranged his material around them. Here's the kicker: Each of the sermons appears to explain and expound the stories that precede them. For instance, the birth narratives of chapters 1–4 answer the question "Who is Jesus?" He is the new Moses, come to save his people. Hence, the first major sermon of the book ('The Sermon on the Mount,' chapters 5–7) portrays Jesus as

> **NOTE:** *It is intriguing to point out that Matthew separates his book into five sections emphasizing Jesus as the new Moses, when the first five books of the Old Testament are considered to have been written by Moses and are commonly called the Pentateuch.*

the new lawgiver. Likewise, chapters 8–9 show Jesus healing and casting out demons as a sign that the least and lost are now invited into the kingdom of God. This is followed by Jesus' second major sermon in chapter 10, where he sends out his Twelve on their first solo flight. This sermon is designed to show that the target audience of the disciples' preaching is the same as Jesus' audience of healings in the previous chapters. So once again, the sermon explains the previous stories. All five of Matthew's sermons function in this way. They really are rather remarkable at highlighting and clarifying the meaning of Jesus' activities.

Revelation is another book with an amazingly intricate structure which revolves around the number seven. After the opening **vision** (1), there are letters to **seven** churches (2–3). This is followed by a **vision** of God's throne room (4–5) followed by **seven** seals and **seven** trumpets (6–9). After this is another

vision of a cosmic battle (10–14) chased by **seven** bowls of wrath (15–16) and a final **vision** of the destiny of Babylon (17–20) and the New Jerusalem (21–22). This is a vast oversimplification. Nonetheless, you get the idea: Revelation revolves around **visions** and **sevens**.

Some books would make very clever screenplays or even theater productions. **Jonah**, for example would be a great action movie with some pretty cool special effects. **Job**, on the other hand, would be a wonderful piece for a reader's theater. And **Song of Songs** could be a stage play, though if it were done accurately, minors would need to be carded at the door! Indeed, there are a variety of literary structures in the Bible, and by tracing them, we will better be able to play mental follow-the-leader with our authors.

Literary Devices within a Book

Aside from these macrostructures that organize whole books, authors use a variety of literary devices *within* their works. It would take years to master all these and probably a bachelor's degree in literature; nonetheless, just by opening our eyes a bit wider, we can catch a great number of them. While they probably won't reveal life-saving theology, they will make the consumption of God's word even sweeter. There are dozens to choose from but the following four will illustrate the point.

An acrostic is when each successive line begins with a different letter so that it creates a pattern. For example, the Greek word for fish is *ixthus*. It became a Christian symbol because each of its letters stands for the first letter of: Jesus, Christ, God, Son, Savior. You may already be familiar with this. Now turn in your Bible to Psalm 119. It is the longest chapter in the Bible with a total of 176 verses. If you will look closely, you will notice that it is divided into eight verse increments. Each verse in every section begins with the same letter of the Hebrew alphabet starting with *aleph* (the first letter) and going through *taw* (the last letter). In fact, if you wanted to learn your Hebrew alphabet, it is printed in your English Bibles, each letter above each section of Psalm 119. Truly, this Psalm is way cooler in Hebrew than it could ever be in

English. This same acrostic pattern is found in Proverbs 31:10–31 and Lamentations 2.

Chiasm is another fascinating device that places texts in parallel positions to create a pattern. It looks like this: A, B, C, D, C', B', A'. The first part of the text and the last part go together, then the second and second-to-last part go together, etc. Matthew 13 is a great example. Here Jesus tells nine parables that stand in chiastic relationship. Check out this outline:

A Sower—Parable on those who hear the word of the kingdom. (vv. 3-9)
  B Disciples' question and Jesus' answer about the purpose of parables and the interpretation of the first parable (vv. 10-23)
    C Tares—Parable on good and evil in the kingdom (vv. 24-30)
      D Mustard seed and leaven—a pair of parallel kingdom parables (vv. 31-35)
        E Jesus leaves the crowd and interprets the tares for the disciples (vv. 36-43).
      D' Treasure and pearl—a pair of parallel kingdom parables (vv. 44-46)
    C' Dragnet—Parable on good and evil in the kingdom (vv. 47-50)
  B' Jesus' question and the disciples' answer about understanding parables (vv. 51-53)
A' Scribe—parable on those trained for the kingdom.

This same kind of chiastic pattern can be found in John 1:1–18:

A ¹In the beginning was the Word, and the Word was with God, and the Word was God. ²He was with God in the beginning.
  B ³Through him all things were made; without him nothing was made that has been made. ⁴In him was life, and that life was the light of men. ⁵The light shines in the darkness, but the darkness has not understood it.
    C ⁶There came a man who was sent from God; his name was John. ⁷He came as a witness to testify concerning that light, so that through him all men might believe.

⁸He himself was not the light; he came only as a witness to the light. ⁹The true light that gives light to every man was coming into the world.

D   ¹⁰He was in the world, and though the world was made through him, the world did not recognize him. ¹¹He came to that which was his own, but his own did not receive him.

    E   ¹²Yet to all who received him, to those who believed in his name, he gave the right to become children of God—¹³children born not of natural descent, nor of human decision or a husband's will, but born of God.

  D' ¹⁴The Word became flesh and made his dwelling among us. We have seen his glory, the glory of the One and Only, who came from the Father, full of grace and truth.

  C' ¹⁵John testifies concerning him. He cries out, saying, "This was he of whom I said, 'He who comes after me has surpassed me because he was before me.'"

B' ¹⁶From the fullness of his grace we have all received one blessing after another. ¹⁷For the law was given through Moses; grace and truth came through Jesus Christ.

A' ¹⁸No one has ever seen God, but God the One and Only, who is at the Father's side, has made him known.

In a chiasm, the very structure emphasizes the central section as the key point the author is trying to get across. It may help to picture the central point of the chiasm like the tip of an arrow—it is the main point!

Parallelism is one of the simplest literary devices and is most common in Hebrew poetry. The author will juxtapose two or more lines to say the same thing, to say the opposite thing, or to build up an argument like steps of a stair. Sometimes, however, this simple device of parallelism will span whole chapters or even books. For example, there is not one creation account in Genesis, there are two: Genesis 1:1–2:3 and Genesis 2:4-25. They are complementary accounts which emphasize different aspects of the creation.

Luke's parallelism doesn't just span chapters, he writes two complementary volumes! One of the most obvious features of his parallelism is in the lives of Peter and Paul. Both healed a lame man (3:6; 14:8f). Peter's shadow and Paul's handkerchief healed people through indirect touch (5:15; 19:12). Both confronted a sorcerer (8:20; 13:8). Both raised the dead (9:36-42; 20:9-12). Both refused to allow someone to worship him (10:25-26; 14:11-15). Both were supported by a Pharisee before the Sanhedrin (5:34-25; 23:6,7). Both were miraculously released from prison (5:19; 16:26). Their visions were both recorded three times (Peter 10:9-23,27-29; 11:4-10; Paul 9:1-19; 22:6-12; 26:12-18). Both were beaten (5:40; 16:22-23). Both were filled with the Holy Spirit (4:8; 9:17; 13:19). Both preached the Word of God with boldness (4:13,31; 9:27-28). And both preached to both Jews and Gentiles (10:34f; 13:46f). OK, that seems pretty obvious. However, you should also notice that most of these also parallel the life of Jesus. It is as if Luke is saying: "So goes Jesus, so goes Peter, so goes Paul." And if you want to know the truth, through the power of the Holy Spirit, so goes *you*.

An *inclusio* is basically a literary sandwich. Two stories on the outside are flavored by the 'meat' on the inside. For example, Genesis 37 and 39 tell the story of Joseph. In chapter 37 he is sold by his brothers to Midianite traders and they pawn him off to Potiphar in Egypt. Chapter 39 continues Joseph's story, telling of his unsuccessful seduction by Potiphar's wife and his ensuing imprisonment. Meanwhile, chapter 38 recounts a couple of R-rated episodes of sexual misconduct in Joseph's family 'back on the farm.' (Read it if you must, but be warned, you will cry, "Yuk!"). The sense one gets when reading these stories together is that Joseph is living a sexually pure life in exile while his family is doing just the opposite in the promised land.

Mark 11:12-25 is another vivid example. This is a wacky tale of Jesus cursing the fig tree. Apparently the curse took place on Monday morning but it was a full twenty-four hours later that the disciples noticed the tree and asked Jesus about it. Sometime later on Monday, Jesus cursed the Temple. Again, you have the story of the fig tree (vv. 12-14,20-25) bracketing the story of the cursing of the Temple (vv. 15-19). However, it is all part of the same story. The cursing of the fig tree is merely an enacted parable in which the unfruitful tree represents the ultimate demise of the Temple and its religious leaders who refuse to bear fruit.

Determining the Purpose of the Book

Once you have marked off the boundaries of your pericope and observed the structure of the book as well as any local literary devices used in shaping your text, there is one last step for fully grasping your context. It is determining the purpose of the book. If you were to find a love-letter in your mother's jewelry box, do you suppose you would respond to it differently if it were signed by your father or if it were signed by your pastor? Unless you are a preacher's kid I dare say that would make a difference! Do you think you would respond differently to a vivid description of a murder if it were a novel as opposed to a police report about your best friend? Would it make a difference if you received a love poem that was on a Hallmark card as opposed to a napkin in the handwriting of your fiancé? Well, duh? The exact same words can have very different meaning based on the purpose of the author and the nature of the book. That's why we must discern the purpose of our book. Here are five ways you can determine that.

1. *The purpose of a book might be overtly stated in the book.* This makes it super easy to figure out why the author wrote the book. For example, John states his purpose in 20:31, "These are written that you may believe that Jesus is the Christ, the Son of God, and that by believing you may have life in his name." Again, Luke introduces his book by saying, ". . . it seemed good also to me to write an orderly account for you, most excellent Theophilus, so that you may know the certainty of the things you have been taught" (1:3b-4). Or how about Solomon's conclusion to Ecclesiastes (12:13): "Now all has been heard; here is the conclusion of the matter: Fear God and keep his commandments, for this is the whole duty of man."

2. *The flow of thought throughout the book may reveal its purpose.* This is certainly true of Genesis. There is a choral refrain throughout the book: "These are the generations . . ." (2:4; 5:1; 6:9; 10:1; 11:10,27; 25:12,19; 36:1,9; 37:2). Clearly the author's goal is to lay out the earliest lineage of Israel from Creation to Abraham and Abraham to Jacob. It moves from Adam to Israel showing God's sovereign plan unfolding in human history.

3. *The occasion for writing the book may suggest its purpose.* For Example, Jeremiah was written against the pressing political backdrop of Nebuchadnezzar's invasion. Mark was likely written in the shadow of Rome during the growth of the Imperial Cult, and Revelation was written a bit later, likely during the persecution by Domitian. Amos 1:1 records the political setting of his book, "The words of Amos, one of the shepherds of Tekoa—what he saw concerning Israel two years before the earthquake, when Uzziah was king of Judah and Jeroboam son of Jehoash was king of Israel." The book of Philemon was prompted when Onesimus, a runaway slave, sought refuge with Paul but was 'returned' by the great Apostle to his friend and brother. Paul exhorted Philemon not to punish his Christian slave since he too was a brother in Christ. We could go on, but these examples suffice to show that the setting of a book can give some significant clues as to the purpose of the work as a whole.

4. *Sometimes the purpose of a book is implied by its contents.* The book of Hebrews demonstrates that Jesus is 'better' and exhorts its readers, therefore, to be faithful to him. Anyone reading Galatians gets the idea pretty quickly that the grace of God is way better than the law. Even a cursory glimpse of Proverbs renders the acquisition of wisdom as its primary purpose. And Ephesians talks so much about the one body of Christ that one must conclude that the unity of Church, both Jew and Gentile, is a significant key to the book. Again, much more could be said, but these examples illustrate how the content of a book will give you a pretty fair idea of its theme(s) and purpose(s).

We can't always know the exact purpose of a book. In fact, some books will have several purposes just like most of your phone conversations or IM's. However, we usually contact other people with one to three things in mind that we want to discuss. If you can figure out the one to three things of a Bible book, you will sharpen your understanding of its overall context and purpose.

Summary

Context is King! There simply is nothing more important in Bible study (nor everyday conversation for that matter) than context. So if you are to understand what your author is saying, first try to establish the parameters of the pericope. Then analyze the structure of the book as a whole as well as any literary devices of your pericope. Seeing the structure will not only allow you to comprehend the contextual meaning of the author, it will also enable you to appreciate the artistry and beauty of his craft. Finally, you should understand why he wrote the book in the first place. What was his purpose? If you can grab these three things—context, structure, and purpose—you will be well on your way to a thorough understanding of the author's intended meaning.

Going Further:

Assignments and Further Reading

Assignment #2:

✍ Using the passage you selected from *Assignment #1*, read through the entire book where your passage is found in one sitting. This will allow you to discern a flow and tone for the book as a whole.

✍ Then, make a general outline of the entire book. Expand the outline in greater detail at the place where your passage is found. Your outline should not have more than 3-5 major headings, or more than 3-5 minor headings under any given point. In addition, include the chapter and verse references alongside each point of the outline for convenience in future assignments.

✍ Finally, in a paragraph or two, explain how your passage fits into the flow of the entire book. To develop this particular observation section, utilize the following questions and some of your own: How does my text fit into the context before and after my pericope(s)? If my text was not written, what would be missing from the whole book? What would be different if my passage were moved to the front or back of the book? Does my passage set up or conclude a major point of the book? Is my text the major point of the book?

Assignment #3:

✍ Complete the following exercise in context:

A STUDY IN CONTEXT

TEXT	OBSERVATIONS	MEANING
Yet man is born to trouble as surely as sparks fly upward. (Job 5:7)	Who is speaking?	
Surely I was sinful at birth, sinful from the time my mother conceived me. (Ps 51:5)	When was this said? With what Genre?	

This is the day the LORD has made; let us rejoice and be glad in it. (Ps 118:24)	See v. 22 & NT usage	
A man can do nothing better than to eat and drink and find satisfaction in his work. This too, I see is from the hand of God. (Eccl 2:24)	Who is speaking and when? Is he cynical in this genre?	
Then I heard the voice of the Lord saying, "Whom shall I send? And who will go for us?" And I said, "Here am I. Send me!" (Isa 6:8)	See vv. 9-13, Is this really a missions text?	
Surely he took up our infirmities and carried our sorrows, yet we considered him stricken by God, smitten by him, and afflicted. (Isa 53:4)	How is this used in the NT? See Matt 8:17.	
"The days are coming," declares the LORD, "when the reaper will be overtaken by the plowman. . . ." (Amos 9:13)	Observe vv. 11-12 and how that is applied in Acts 15:16-18.	
For where two or three come together in my name, there am I with them. (Matt 18:20)	Observe vv. 16-20; cf. Deut 17:6	
The Counselor, the Holy Spirit . . . will teach you all things and will remind you of everything I have said to you. (John 14:26)	Who is speaking to whom? When?	
Everyone who calls on the name of the Lord will be saved. (Acts 2:21)	Where is this quote from? See vv. 38ff.	
I can do all things through him who gives me strength. (Phil 4:13)	see vv. 10-12, 14-17	
If we are faithless, he will remain faithful, for he cannot disown himself. (2 Tim 2:13)	Does this support eternal security? See v. 12.	
And if anyone takes words away from this book or prophecy, God will take away from him his share in the tree of life and in the holy city, which are described in this book. (Rev 22:19)	Is "this book" Revelation or the whole Bible?	

Further Reading:

✍ Listen to Mark Moore's lectures on context at: http://markmoore.org/resources/lectures.html

  ✍ Listen to all three—Context: Part 1, Part 2, and Part 3

✍ Explore www.biblestudytools.net to get familiar with the amazing amount of resources they offer, which will become vital for the future assignments. This website has everything from concordance tools, commentaries, sermon helps, to a nifty parallel tool for looking at different translations of a single verse. Add five more websites to your Bible Study Favorites.

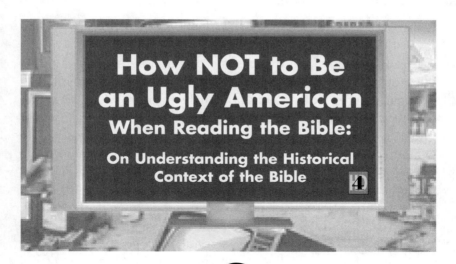

How NOT to Be an Ugly American
When Reading the Bible:
On Understanding the Historical Context of the Bible

4

Once while I was speaking at a conference in Latin America, I attempted to practice my Spanish by starting a conversation with a group of high school students sitting in the lunchroom. I waited in line for food while they were seated at a table next to me. As the line passed by them, I tapped each one on the head and said, "Pato, Pato, Pato . . . Gonso." Translated this means "Duck, duck, duck . . . goose." Are you familiar with this game? It is a children's game where everyone sits in a circle except the one who is 'it.' The 'it' person taps each head as s/he walks around the circle repeating the word 'duck.' When s/he finally taps a person and says 'goose,' the chase is on. The 'goose' tries to get up off the ground, run around the circle and catch the 'it' before 'it' makes it around to the goose's little nest and settle's into the open space. Now I was relatively certain that these Latino teens knew nothing of my little game. But that was the point! I wanted to start a conversation. Boy, did I! I turned around to see their faces after labeling a number of them ducks and one of them a goose. They stared at me with these horrified looks. Clearly I had said something very wrong. So in my broken Spanish and in their broken English I explained the game to them while they explained that in their particular country the word 'duck' was a slang term for a homosexual. So there I was, a preacher at this Christian conference where I called a number of *machismo* Latin teens "queer" and one of them I identified as a goose. Oh, the joys of being an idiot in multiple languages!

So let me help you avoid some of the more egregious errors internationally. If you go to the Orient, don't point with your feet—in some cultures that's a way of identifying a prostitute. Likewise, you should never beckon someone to come to you by pulling your finger toward yourself with your palm up. It basically means the same thing as pointing your feet at someone. If you get to Chile and someone across the room purses her lips as if to kiss you (don't flatter yourself, she's not making an offer), it is just their way of pointing. In India, always shake with the *right* hand. The left is reserved for an act of personal hygiene that you might find a bit shocking. In Africa, don't eat everything on your plate, otherwise they

> One's destination is never a place, but a new way of seeing things."
> —Henry Miller

will fill it up again. In Europe, don't expect a lot of ice in your drinks (even if you ask) and don't expect your bill in a restaurant *until* you ask. They would *never* rush you out of the restaurant by giving you a bill; that would just be rude!

The list of cultural peculiarities could go on and on. That's why it is always a good idea to pick up a guidebook whenever you are taking a trip overseas. It will tell you the best places to eat, the best means of transportation, and the major sights to see. It will also warn you about particular dangers you might face as well as any cultural *faux pas* you might need to avoid. This chapter is like one of those travel guides. We are inviting

> If you reject the food, ignore the customs, fear the religion and avoid the people, you might better stay at home."
> —James Michener

you to take a trip with us to the biblical world. We hope to help you avoid some of the bigger pitfalls while on foreign soil.

What to Look for in Cultural Background

When we are investigating the historical or cultural background of a text there are dozens of things one could look for (fortunately, they are all fabulously interesting). You might think they don't much matter for the understanding of a text, but let's look at a few random examples:

Dress: Does it really matter what people wore? It mattered to a woman with a gynecological problem in Luke 8:44. She wanted to be healed, and so she touched the 'edge' of Jesus' cloak in order to be made well. This par-ticular word is used of the tassels which were found on the four corners of a Jewish prayer shawl. If Jesus dressed like a kosher Jew, he surely would have worn one. These tassels were knotted in specific ways, and each knot repre-sented a prayer the man would say (similar to Catholic rosary beads). There was a superstition common in Jesus' day that a righteous man's prayers left a kind of invisible, spiritual 'pixie dust' on these tassels as he fingered them with each of his daily prayers. This woman apparently thought that if she could physically lay hold of the tassel, she would mystically contact his prayer power and be healed. Apparently, clothes do matter.

Plants: While Jesus was on the cross, one of the soldiers put a sponge on a 'hyssop' branch and lifted it to Jesus' mouth (John 19:29). Since crucifixion victims were normally not more than a foot and a half off the ground, it didn't need to be a long 'stick.' The problem, however, is that hyssop is too flimsy to hold a sponge soaked with wine even if it only needed to extend it 18". The fact is that hyssop is more of an herb than a shrub. It makes

a better paint brush than it does a pole. So why does the Bible say this stick was made of hyssop? Well, hyssop, like 'Kleenex,' was used as kind of a 'brand name' for any 'stick' that fit the category. Hence, 'hyssop' could represent a twig of any genus. So John uses the 'brand name' rather than the actual genus. Why? Was he botanically challenged? Surely not. Rather, he is speaking theologically rather than scientifically. Remember hyssop makes a great paint brush. That was exactly its purpose for sprinkling blood on the altar during the Day of Atonement or pure water to cleanse utensils in the temple (cf.

Exod 12:22; Lev 14:4,6; Num 19:18, etc.). John, so very Jewish in his scriptural allusions, uses this peculiar word for 'stick' to remind us that something deeper is happening here on the cross.

Construction: Matthew, Mark, and Luke all tell about a paralytic whose friends let him through the roof—not without a good bit of demolition (Matt 9:2-9//Mark 2:3-12//Luke 5:18-26). Mark says they "made an opening in the roof." In other words, they dug through the thatch and mud, no doubt making quite a mess, until Jesus could sunbathe. Luke, on the other hand, says they removed the 'ceramic tiles.' So which is it, tiles or thatch? Actually, Mark has it right. That's because he lived in Palestine and knew how houses were actually constructed. Luke, on the other hand, is writing for Theophilus. He lived in the West where roofs were made from ceramic tiles. It isn't that Luke is *wrong* per se, he is just rewording the scene so the picture of the house makes sense to his reader(s).

Literature: We call them Epistles (no, they are not wives of the Apostles). They are letters. In fact, the letters of the New Testament compare remarkably well to historical examples of letters from Rome or Egypt. The structure, however, is very different from ours. Let's review Business Forms 101: What goes first on a letter? Well, the date, then four spaces and the return address. Then you put "Dear So-and-so," and you're off and running. Then, after all is said, you write, "Sincerely, ME." Now, when you get a letter, what is the first thing you look for? That's right! You go to the bottom of the letter to see who it is from. Letters should *start*, not end, with the author. And if you look at each of the letters of the New Testament, that is exactly what you will find. There is much more to say here, but it will have to wait until we talk about the various forms of literature we find in the Bible.

Money: How about just one more example? Jesus was accosted by the Herodians and Pharisees (strange political bedfellows to be sure). They asked him if it was right to pay taxes to Caesar or not. Oh my, that's a trap! If he says, "Yes, pay your taxes," the crowds will abandon him. After all, they were hoping for a political liberator. But if he says, "No, don't pay your taxes," the Herodians would have immediately cuffed him. So what does he do? He asks for a denarius. It was a small coin worth a day's wages to a com-

Tiberias

Livia

mon soldier. Almost everyone had them. But that, precisely, was the problem! These little coins were *blasphemous!* On the front of the coin was a picture of the current emperor, Tiberius (you really should know about him . . . what a mess!). He had a saying inscribed around the coin in Latin abbreviations: Tiberius Caesar, son of the Divine Augustus. That is going to choke any Jewish Rabbi quicker than bacon. On the back of the coin is his mother sitting on the throne of a goddess with the words *'pontif maxim'* = high priest. Jesus is absolutely brilliant. One glance at the coin and a brief little "humphhh" would say everything he needed to: "Get rid of the idolatry in your pocket and let God alone rule your lives." Brilliant!

Knowing the historical background is like seeing these stories in color rather than merely black and white. You can still understand the story of a black and white movie, but the color version is a lot more appealing. We could offer innumerable examples of weddings, funerals, dance, mourning, tools, literature, war, etiquette, agriculture, employment, taxation, religion, holidays, economics, etc. These historical items might fall under three primary categories.

First, one must consider issues of **history** such as political rulers, dates, governmental offices, etc. What do you know about the political rulers of Jesus' day? Were you aware that Tiberius Caesar was one of the worst of all the Emperors and the first to demand worship as a god in his own lifetime? Did you know that Pilate was a racist, especially against the Jews? Herod the Great had two of his own son's strangled. Hillel, the great Rabbi who first drew up rules of hermeneutics, likely died the year Jesus went into the temple at age 12. Nero assassinated Peter and Paul the very same year he himself was forced to commit suicide. These facts are not recorded in the Bible but are inscribed in the history books of the day. By knowing a bit of history the Bible has greater depth and sharper contours. But how can one learn all this stuff? Hold on for just a minute; we'll get to that.

Second, one should consider issues of **culture**. These would include questions pertaining to social customs, values, and traditions. Did you know that approximately 92% of the population lived hand to mouth on the brink of starvation every day? Or that barley was the grain for the poor and wheat the choice of the rich? Are you aware that Jewish men sometimes wore earrings and Jewish women nose rings? Is it news to you that the Year of Jubilee was probably never actually practiced? Fact: women were not generally allowed to give testimony in a court of law. Here's another interesting tidbit: Jews were more likely to have a goose as a pet than a dog. The most honorable Roman occupation was farming. If you had to relieve yourself in Rome one of the best places was the Laundromat because urine was used as part of the solution to clean clothes. (And, yes, without washing machines, certain slaves were assigned to 'churn' the clothes by walking through the vats of this solution).

Third, one should learn about the **environment**. What did Jesus mean when he said, "It will be fair weather, for the sky is red"? And why did people *always* go 'up' to Jerusalem, even when coming from the north (hint: they walked)? Oh, how about this one: Which animal was the most efficient means of transporting goods: camel, horse (with a cart), donkey, ox (with a cart)?[1] Which was the most common method of assassination in the first century: drowning, poisoning, crucifixion, or burning?[2] Why are there no poisonous snakes today on Malta when Paul got bit by one there? And why did David kill a bear and a lion if neither of those animals are in Israel today (perhaps PETA could help)?

Culture Shock!

We live in a very different world than the Bible. To illustrate, let's do this little exercise. In the space below, make a list of every-

---

[1] If you said, "donkey" you are correct. The roads were so rough that a cart was very difficult to maneuver and would break with heavy loads.
[2] Poisoning . . . which leads me to ask, "Do you know what plants you can eat with John the Baptist out in the wilderness?"

thing that would freak Paul out if he were to suddenly rise from the dead and spend a week with you.

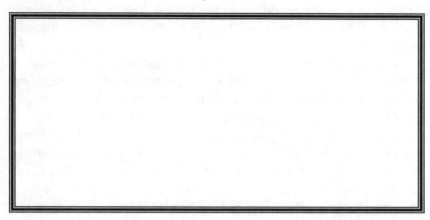

Here is my own list with which you can compare yours: (1) Paul would be shocked at the relationships between men and women. Their open communication and physical touch would border on the scandalous. Female politicians, soldiers, police officers, and teachers would all be outrageous for the Apostle. (2) The amount of money we have and how we horde it would be mind-boggling to the great Apostle. You see, in the ancient world money was primarily good for one thing—giving away so as to gain honor. To lose honor to gain money would seem, to Paul, counterintuitive. He would have to wonder why Christians with rampant wealth would not think to use it to extend the fame of Jesus. (3) Our individualism would appear foolish since he was weaned in corporate culture. Our passion for solitude, privacy, personal rights, and individual expression wouldn't just be selfish; it would be unwise, undesirable, and unsafe. (4) Our emphasis on entertainment rather than social development would simply mystify Paul. Not just the hours we spend looking at television, but the whole gamut of iPods, cinema, text messages, sports teams, etc. would surely be downright dizzying. (5) The separation of the sacred and secular he might label blasphemous unbelief; the construction of so many church buildings he might consider a throwback to temples made with hands; our fear of ridicule for our faith he surely would scorn as radical infidelity to the Master who so suffered on our behalf. (6) He would probably rightly marvel at our educational systems; technological advances for evangelism; the fact that so many in the world claim the name of Jesus; and a government that attempted to serve the poor rather than abuse them as slave labor.

Our lists could be much longer, of course. Yet this much is ample evidence that we need to ask some questions about the background of the text. At this point my greatest gift to you would be a reporter's pad and a pencil. Here are the questions that will keep you on fertile soil in historical background: Who? What? When? Where? Why? How? And quit looking just on the surface (don't be so boring). Peek behind the pages of the text. See who's lurking in the shadows. Lift up the mattress and dig in the back

> *The two greatest tools for Bible study are (1) a child's curiosity and (2) a pencil and paper.*

yard. Find out what this passage is hiding. This is like CSI! You gotta pay attention to things that normal people miss. How? Well, just be patient and we will map it out clearly in a moment.

First, *why* should you be concerned about the historical background of a text? (1) *A text cannot mean what it never meant.* This is simply to say that if you apply a passage to a contemporary setting that goes beyond what Paul would affirm to his own audience, then you have not interpreted the text; you have manipulated it. Or to put it another way: If you say to Paul, "This is what you meant when you said _____" and he looks back at you and says, "Huh?" then you are wrong. So before we apply the text in the 21st century we had better retrieve it from the 1st century.

(2) *Christianity is historically based.* This is true of very few religions. For instance, if Mohammed never actually existed, the tenets of Islam would still be valid. The same can be said for Confucius, Buddha, and Sung Young Moon. However, if Jesus never existed, Christianity is a misguided superstition that we would do well to abandon. It just plain matters whether the biblical stories hap-

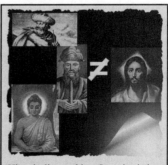

Historically speaking, Jesus is vital to Christianity in a manner that is unparalleled in all the other major religions.

pened or not; it just plain matters whether we see it for what it *was* before making it what it *is*.

(3) *Knowing history will allow you to read the Bible in color rather than black and white.* Take a moment and read Psalm 51 armed with the knowledge that David had just been caught by Nathan the prophet in adultery and murder. Read Philippians 4:4-7 in light of the historical fact that Paul had just been in prison for two years in Caesarea and was now in the middle of a two-year sentence of house-arrest in Rome. Read Luke 9:23 reflecting on the fact that Romans only crucified foreigners they disdained and that most Jews of Jesus' day had likely witnessed at least one execution by crucifixion in their lifetimes. One more, read Mark 14:12-14, against the backdrop of a chauvinistic culture where men did NOT do women's work (like carrying water).

(4) Finally, *you cannot properly understand the New Testament without understanding the Old Testament.* This is true for EVERY book in the New Testament (well, OK, you *might* get away with reading Philemon without knowing Moses). There are 295 Old Testament passages cited in 352 different New Testament verses (some obviously cited multiple times).[3] Moreover, hundreds of allusions to the Old Testament are scattered across every New Testament book. It is estimated that over 500 Old Testament allusions are in the 404 verses of Revelation alone. The Old Testament is thus the *assumed* background of the NT, and those unfamiliar with it are at an automatic disadvantage. It's kind of like going to an opera or a cricket match. If you don't know the language or the rules, you are hopelessly lost and inevitably bored. That is not because cricket and opera are boring (obviously millions of people are fans), but because we are ignorant. So also, many find the Old Testament boring. How can that be?! We see battles and blood, poetry and romance, miracles, and assassinations. It has more action than the Lord of the Rings trilogy and parts are even rated R (and not for 'Righteous'). Our disinterest in the OT says more about our narrow view than its shallow contents. With this

---

[3] Roger Nicole, "New Testament Use of the Old Testament," *Revelation and the Bible*, ed. by Carl. F.H. Henry (Grand Rapids: Baker, 1958) 137-151 [http://www.bible-researcher.com/nicole.html].

in mind, let us now turn to the important task of learning how to travel to the biblical world.

How to Access the Historical Background of a Text

There is hardly anything better than a cool story, and the Bible is chock full of them. But what makes them super-cool is when a teacher can unpack the historical details surrounding them. There are basically three sources from which to glean historical background information. The problem is that all three sources require extensive reading. Furthermore, the unfortunate fact is that most of what you will read will be neither exciting nor interesting. You may have to read ten or twenty pages before finding that really cool nugget. This is the nature of mining. You do a lot of digging through dirt and rock before finding precious metal. Patience, however, *inevitably* pays off. There is no shortcut for historical research. You must read, especially in the original sources, and read a lot. If you do, however, you will begin to build a cultural and historical portfolio that you can use for years to come in making the Bible come alive. OK, so here's what you've been waiting for: the three sources for historical investigation.

First, your best historical source is **the Bible** *itself.* It is a big fat book with lots of stories and all of them are in a Jewish, middle-eastern setting. That is our target area and so the Bible becomes your greatest historical source. Let's say you want to study shepherding: Who were shepherds? What were their duties? Were they respected? How well were they paid? etc. Just start searching the Scriptures for clues. In John 10, for example, Jesus speaks of his shepherding role of calling the sheep by name, protecting them from predators and robbers, putting them in their pen at night, and being the 'door to the sheep' which required laying in the opening of the low rock wall. We also learn that hired hands will flee in the face of danger and sometimes kill the sheep themselves to eat them. True owners, on the other hand, will organize search parties for wayward sheep, lay down their lives for their sheep, lead them to still waters, and separate them from goats (cf. Psalm 23; Ezekiel 34; Zechariah 11). The information

This photo shows a few sheep in a typical 'pen' in Jordan. Its walls are broken down, but you can still see to the upper right the opening or 'door' where the shepherd would lay at night.

is there in the Bible if we are willing to take the time to search it out through concordance work.

Second, your reading of the Bible should be augmented with a **Bible Dictionary** *or a* **Bible Encyclopedia** (really the only difference between the two is their relative length—encyclopedias are longer and more comprehensive). Look up your topic (alphabetically) and see what an expert in the field has to say about **a**griculture, **b**uilding, **c**hildren, **d**ogs, **e**ast, **f**asting, **g**oats, **h**ealing . . . **X**erxes, **y**outh, **Z**edekiah. These dictionaries and encyclopedias can be very expensive. Don't be fooled by the latest edition with the new color pictures on the cover. Ninety-nine percent of the information in the old edition is identical to the new. Want my advice? Buy a computer concordance that has one of these embedded in it. It won't be the newest, but it will have about ten times more information than you will ever use anyway. Another option is simply to access the good material that has been made available online for free.[4]

---

[4] For a fine **Dictionary,** see http://eastonsbibledictionary.com/ or http://www.bible-history.com/smiths/. For an **Encyclopedia**, go to: http://www.studylight.org/enc/isb/ or http://www.christiananswers.net/dictionary/home.html.

In addition to dictionaries and/or encyclopedias, *you should look for an **Atlas*** to help you locate places on a map. However, you should no longer be satisfied with two-dimensional maps like you find in the back of your study Bible. You should find maps that show topography, distance, and even weather conditions, such as the satellite images available through GoogleEarth or NASA's collection of satellite photos of the Middle East.[5] Furthermore, there are fine sources for free Bible maps online that can be downloaded and used for study and teaching purposes. In addition to maps, however, you should augment your study with the plethora of **photographs** that are available online.[6] With all the sources available at your fingertips for free, how dare you be boring in your Bible study. May boring Bible students be smitten with the curse of a camel's halitosis! Finally, there are a host of sites that look at the latest and best discoveries of **archaeology** and how this science confirms the Bible's historical, cultural, and geographical references.[7]

*Third, beyond the Bible, you should read other **historical works** from the biblical period.* These will fall under several categories.

(1) **Apocryphal books**, most of which were written between the Testaments. There are thirteen books of varying historical value which the Catholic Church deemed worthy to include in the canon.[8] While there are good reasons for not considering them Scripture, there is *no* good reason for excluding them from our sources for

---

[5] For Google Earth see http://earth.google.com/ and for NASA's photos go to http://visibleearth.nasa.gov/view_set.php?categoryID=2116. For a standard Bible **Atlas**, see http://www.biblemap.org/, or http://www.bible-history.com/maps/. For a virtual tour of Jerusalem you can access http://www.md.huji.ac.il/vjt/.

[6] For photos of Israel and the Ancient Near East, see http://freestockphotos.com/.

[7] For a couple of the best archaeological sites see http://www.biblicalarchaeology.org/ and http://www.biblicalarcheology.net/.

[8] The Old Testament **Apocrypha** is available online at http://wesley.nnu.edu/biblical_studies/noncanon/apocrypha.htm. In addition you might look at the Old Testament **Pseudepigrapha**: http://wesley.nnu.edu/biblical_studies/noncanon/pseudepigrapha.htm. While it has less historical value, it is still of much interest.

historical background. In fact, in terms of describing the historical setting of the biblical period, these books are as valuable as Scriptures themselves.

(2) **Greco-Roman writers**, who are (roughly) contemporaneous with the biblical authors. The most important historians would include Josephus[9] (37–95 C.E.), Tacitus (55–117 C.E.), Suetonius (c. 70–130 C.E.), Livy (c. 59 B.C.E.–17 C.E.), Appian (c. 95–165 C.E.), Herodotus (c. 484–425 B.C.E.) and Xenophon (c. 430–355 B.C.E.). But we can also benefit from helpful philosophers such as Philo[10] (c. 20 B.C.E.–50 C.E.), Seneca (c. 4 B.C.E.–65 C.E.), and Epictetus (c. 55–135 C.E.). Yet this is just the tip of the proverbial iceberg. You can peruse and enjoy literally tens of thousands of pages of ancient documents. Good thing for you that they are almost all available online for free *and searchable* both in English and their original Greek or Latin![11] (We live in great times for Bible study!)

You might think that these writings are too far off, too hard to understand, and too hard to incorporate into your understanding of the Bible. But how can you possibly know that without reading a few dozen pages from several of them? Please allow me to give you just two examples of how important they can be. The following is an excerpt from Josephus's *Antiquities* 18.63–64, where he

Apocryphal Books
Tobit (200 B.C.E.)
Judith (C.E. 150)
Additions to Esther (130 B.C.E.)
Wisdom of Solomon (30 B.C.E.)
Ecclesiasticus (32 B.C.E.)
Baruch (C.E. 100)
Epistle of Jeremiah (200 B.C.E.)
Prayer of Ahazariah (100 B.C.E.)
Story of Suzanna (100 B.C.E.)
Bel & the Dragon (100 B.C.E.)
1 Maccabees (110 B.C.E.)
2 Maccabees (100 B.C.E.)
Prayer of Manasseh (150 B.C.E.)

[9] The works of **Josephus** can easily be found on the internet, but my favorite site is http://pace.cns.yorku.ca/York/york/texts.htm, because it allows you to access the Greek as well as the English edition, and it allows you to locate passages using either of the two major numbering systems used in scholarly literature.

[10] **Philo's** works are available at http://www.earlyjewishwritings.com/philo.html.

[11] The Perseus site is simply a wonder to behold. While it can be a bit slow and stubborn at times, the wealth of original **Greek and Latin** sources here is mind-boggling: http://www.perseus.tufts.edu/cache/perscoll_Greco-Roman.html.

describes Jesus. It has likely been altered by a Christian editor (indicated by the italics), but here is what he says:

> Now there was about this time Jesus, a wise man, *if it be lawful to call him a man*; for he was a doer of wonderful works, a teacher of such men as receive the truth with pleasure. He drew over to him both many of the Jews and many of the Gentiles. *He was [the] Christ.* And when Pilate, at the suggestion of the principal men amongst us, had condemned him to the cross, those that loved him at the first did not forsake him; *for he appeared to them alive again the third day; as the divine prophets had foretold these and ten thousand other wonderful things concerning him.* And the tribe of Christians, so named from him, are not extinct at this day.

This simple statement yields a great deal of insight into one of the earliest Jewish views of Jesus. Likewise, the following statement from Tacitus confirms Jesus' death by crucifixion under Pontius Pilate: "*Christus*, from whom the name had its origin, suffered the extreme penalty during the reign of Tiberius at the hands of one of our procurators, Pontius Pilatus," (*Annals* 15.44). Hundreds of examples like these could be cited to show how much the historical background of the Bible is confirmed and clarified by Greco-Roman authors.

(3) Volumes of **Jewish writings** emerged after the first century. The most important are the **Talmud, Mishnah, Targum** and **Midrash.** The *Mishnah* is simply a collection of Jewish oral laws from the Rabbis spanning hundreds of years both before and after Jesus. The Mishnah was eventually written down, along with its commentary (Gemara), in two editions which are now called the Jerusalem *Talmud* and the Babylonian *Talmud*, codified between the 3rd and 5th century C.E.[12] The *Targumim* are basically Aramaic paraphrases of the Old Testament which give us an idea of the variety of interpretations and interests of Judaism in the centuries surrounding Jesus' life.[13] And the *Midrashim* are various

---

[12] The Babylonian **Talmud** is available at http://www.jewishvirtuallibrary.org/jsource/Talmud/talmudtoc.html.

[13] The two main **Targumim**, Pseudo-Jonathan and Onkelos, are available at http://www.targum.info/pj/psjon.htm.

exegetical expositions that include sermons, stories, and maxims that illustrate and expound on the Jewish laws.[14] The **Qumran** scrolls also represent a wealth of material contemporary with Jesus and from the same geographic area. However, they are from a sect which isolated itself from society at large and thus it is difficult to know how much of their views Jesus and the Apostles might have shared. This material has not yet been made available online, although there are a number of very good English translations.[15]

Don't kid yourself. These Jewish documents are lengthy, diverse, esoteric, and paradoxical. As one Rabbi told me: "If you ask three Rabbis their opinion on any point you will get five answers." So don't think that any given Rabbinic statement was the definitive view of Judaism. Nonetheless, these writings will shed light on the cultural and especially theological landscape of early Judaism. What makes them so difficult, however, aside from their diversity, is the fact that much of it was writ-ten hundreds of years after Jesus and more importantly after the destruction of the Temple. Judaism went through massive transforma-tions during that period, so it is difficult to say which opinions, views, and laws were available to Jesus or would have poten-tially impacted him. These docu-ments are harder to access, more difficult to understand, and more complex to analyze than those mentioned previously. Personally, I would not recommend diving into them just yet. I mention them

This is a picture of the Dome of the Rock (the Muslim holy place built between A.D. 687 and 691 by the 9th Caliph). This structure is built directly on top of the temple destroyed in A.D. 70. (picture taken by Jordan Wood in July 2007)

here not so that you will go out and read them. Rather, I mention them so that you will be aware of their existence and pay atten-

---

[14] Some of the **Midrashim** are available at http://www.sacred-texts.com/jud/tmm/index.htm.

[15] My pick is Geza Vermes, *The Complete Dead Sea Scrolls in English* (New York: Penguin Books, 1997).

tion when scholars use them. This is the deep end of the theological pool—don't drown in this material before you have mastered much of the other material.

(4) Finally, the **Early Church Fathers** offer Christian perspectives on the Bible, theology, and culture, which span the years 100 C.E. onward. Again, this material is diverse and voluminous. Don't get lost in it. While it is easier to access than the Jewish material, and while it is more familiar to you as a Christian, you still need to be aware that this material is a *development of Christian theology*. That is to say, new cultural challenges sometimes forced new ways of dealing with theological issues and church government. Hence, you ought not to say, "Irenaeus said . . ." or "Origen believed . . ." without knowing when he said this, to whom, and under what circumstances. You should also keep in mind that this is not historical *background* for the Bible, but historical *foreground.* The church fathers followed historically, culturally, and sociologically the world of the Bible. With these cautions in mind, however, this material can be immensely valuable as we look at how history flowed from the biblical world and toward our own western world. One of the wonderful things about this material is that it is available online and is searchable.[16] This is especially helpful for theological topics when you are attempting to see how a verse or idea was understood by the earliest Christian teachers.

Conclusion

It would not have been possible to write this chapter two years ago, and in another two years it will need to be revised. The reason is that volumes of valuable original material are being uploaded daily. These materials allow you to read Greek, Roman, and Jewish sources which are roughly contemporaneous with the biblical world. Thus, you are permitted a peek into the culture, politics, geography, and society of the Bible, enabling you to read

---

[16] The entire collection of **Early Church Fathers** is available online at http://www.ccel.org/fathers.html

with a clearer perspective. There is no longer any excuse for imposing our own cultural values on Scripture. We have the materials available for a sensitive, and frankly, a far more interesting view. You are now able to travel back in time and across vast continents. I hope you enjoy the natives as well as the views. Have a great trip.

Going Further:

Assignments and Further Reading

Assignment #4:

✍ Read the introductions of two commentaries on the book in which your passage is found. You will want to be able to tell the purpose/theme of your book, the author, the date, the destination, and any occasion that might have prompted the writing of that book. Some key questions to guide you in your reading include: Who wrote the book? What was the author's background? What was the date of writing for the book? What was the nature of the author's ministry at this point in his life? What was the author's relationship with the original audience of the letter? Why was the author writing the book? Who was the writer writing to? What was their background? What was happening to them at the time the author wrote the book? What was the relationship the audience had to God? to each other? What was happening in the world at the time of the book's writing?

✍ In addition, identify any key words or recurring phrases in the book. Often times these recurrences can clue the reader in to the answers to the previous questions.

✍ If you do not have access to a library full of biblical commentaries, then refer to the internet links below for online resources:
   ☛ http://cf.blueletterbible.org/commentaries/
   ☛ http://www.bibletexts.com/
   ☛ http://www.rickysoo.com/mhcc/
   ☛ http://www.biblestudytools.net/Commentaries/
   ☛ http://www.mybibletools.com/bible/commentaries.htm

Assignment #5:

✍ Make a photocopy of your text, and do the following to the replica: (a) Highlight specific items that you think will require historical research. In the margins write out the kinds of historical questions you would want to have answered about your text, which you will look to answer in the following assignment. (b) Also in the margins, list other passages which mention your highlighted items.

Assignment #6:

✍ Using a Bible encyclopedia or dictionary, write a brief paragraph on each item of your internal historical setting that you circled in project 5(a). This paragraph should basically answer the kinds of questions you wrote in the margin about those historical items.

✍ If you do not have access to a library full of biblical dictionaries or biblical encyclopedias at your disposal, then refer to the internet links below for online resources:
  ☞ Dictionaries:
    ☞ http://www.biblestudytools.net/Dictionaries/
    ☞ http://www.eastons-bible-dictionary.com/eastons/bible-study.htm
    ☞ http://speedbibledictionary.com/
  ☞ Encyclopedias:
    ☞ http://www.bibliapedia.com/forum/bibliapedia.php
    ☞ http://www.christiananswers.net/dictionary/home.html
    ☞ http://apmethodist.org/biblestudy.htm

Oh, My Word!

5

"When words are scarce they are seldom spent in vain,"
William Shakespeare

"Words are only postage stamps delivering the object for you to unwrap,"
George Bernard Shaw

"One great use of words is to hide our thoughts,"
Voltaire

Words are just plain fascinating. To illustrate the point, let's simply define the word 'word.' Technically a 'word' is "the smallest unit of speech with independent meaning" or "a group of letters arranged in a specific pattern to form a linguistic symbol representing an idea." So far that is straightforward enough. However, figuratively 'word' can mean a message (such as "a word from our sponsor" (cf. Gal 5:14) or a promise ("I give you my word"). It can even mean 'news' or 'tidings' ("She sent word") or in an exalted sense it refers to Scripture as 'God's Word.' This message of God was then personified in Jesus who is the 'Word' (John 1:1). It takes an entire paragraph to define the word "word"! Furthermore, this does not take into account all the idioms using the word 'word': "Oh, my word," "Woooord," "His word is good," "What's the good word?" "She's too wordy," "I've not heard a word," "Not another word out of you," "Keep your word," "Empty words," "Without words," and on it goes.

So this chapter will be devoted to helping you grab hold of the meaning of words. However, the dissection of an author's thoughts down to the basic building block of words is only helpful insofar as it enables the interpreter to *reconstruct* with accuracy the larger framework of the author's ideas.

> **CAUTION:**
> *An author's meaning is not in words, nor even in sentences, but rather in paragraphs.*

Linguistic Tangent (for those of you curious about how language works): From the smallest unit to the largest, here is how language is built:

> letter < morpheme¹ < word < sentence < pericope/ paragraph < unit/discourse/chapter < book.

A **letter** is an arbitrary symbol that differs from language to language. It means nothing by itself (except of course for those rare single letter words such as 'I' [very popular in English] and 'a'). A **morpheme**, likewise, is meaningless without its connection to a full word. After all, one would be thought silly if she walked into a room and said: "I am ing with an un ing ic self ab ed un ful pig." But if you fill in the blanks it becomes a rather informative piece of communication: "I am living with an unloving, egocentric, self-absorbed, ungrateful pig." So *words are the smallest unit of language with real meaning.* However, words

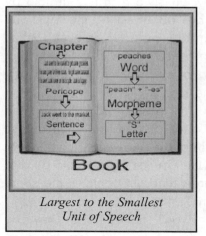

Largest to the Smallest Unit of Speech

---

¹ A morpheme is a group of letters with independent meaning. For example, 'independent' is made up of three morphemes: in/depend/ent. The first means 'not' also expressed by the morphemes 'un' and 'a' or sometimes 'mis'. 'Depend' means to be reliant on or connected to or figuratively as an option 'that depends.' Finally the word ends in 'ent' making it an adjective. There are hundreds of these little fellows in the English language and we have become so familiar with them that we hardly think twice about the roles they play.

outside of a sentence are relatively incomprehensible. For example take the simple word, "Hey." What does that mean? That depends entirely on what follows it: "Hey, jerk" (said in a Wal-Mart checkout line); "Hey, stop" (said by a sibling); "Hey, you" (said by a flirting cheerleader); "Hey, there" (said by a policeman to his partner). This illustrates why words, without sentences are worthless.

Remember this lesson as we proceed to talk about how to do word studies. Understanding the meaning of a Greek or Hebrew word in the Bible will NOT help you understand the author's intended meaning unless you know how it functions in the sentence and on the lips of the one who uses it. In fact, even sentences are relatively meaningless unless put in the broader context of a train of thought called a paragraph (or technically a 'pericope'). For example, if you read "You surely shall not die," what does this mean? When we read this phrase in Genesis 3:4, it is a lie told by Satan to Eve about eating the fruit. She and Adam did die. In 2 Samuel 19:23, it was a promise of David to Shimei that he would not execute him for previously cursing the king. In Numbers 18:32, the phrase is part of the instructions to the priest; if they carried out their duties

> **Pericope:** *"a chunk of text with meaning,"* roughly equivalent to a paragraph but its boundaries are marked not by indentations but by the actual beginning and ending of a major idea.

properly in the temple, they would not die. However, the implications is, of course, if they failed in their duties there would be dire consequences indeed. In these three different contexts the same sentence means three very different things.

Exhortation: Dive into these word studies hard. They are fascinating and terribly rewarding. You are going to *love* this exercise. But never, never, never forget that the purpose is always to understand the author's intended meaning and this cannot be done by being a linguistic expert, but only by putting these words into sentences and then reading the sentences in the context of the broader argument. With that said, let's get down to business.

Preliminary Considerations

In the city of Seattle there is the famous Pike Street Fish Market where the workers have a ball. "How," you might ask, "could workers who sell raw, stinky fish enjoy their jobs?!" You would really have to visit Pike Street to fully appreciate this, but a group of workers took a crummy, smelly job and turned it into a game. Whenever someone orders a fish, they shout out the order and the other workers echo back: "Salmon" or "Pike" or whatever the specified aquatic creature. Then they start throwing the fish forward to the checkout counter somewhat like infielders in baseball throw the ball around the bases after an out. They never drop the slippery fish for they have mastered the art of catching slimy fish. Often they will toss these deceased beasts to the customers themselves who invariable experience the slippery beast shooting through their fingers. There is an art to catching slippery fish. Likewise, this little game we play in catching the meaning of words will take some practice, for words are slippery little things. Before trying to grab hold of them, let me give you seven preliminary considerations (insider tips if you will) that will help you master the art of catching slippery words.

1. Words have both denotation and connotation. Just because you know what the dictionary says about a word does not mean you know what an author means. Pretend, for example, that you are an Arab immigrant to the US and trying to understand the new world in which you find yourself. You hear someone say, "That's cheesy." When she is talking about

> **Denotation:** *The dictionary definition of a word.*
> **Connotation:** *The implications or emotions a word carries in actual use.*

some chips, that's one thing, but when she is describing your joke, that is something entirely different. On any given day our Arab immigrant is likely to hear: "That's bad, man." "Too cool." "Out of sight!" "Sweet!" "Get out!" "He's hot." "What up?" "I'm starving." "Pimp my ride." Or thousands of other idioms. You can imagine my consternation the first time I ordered water in the Middle East and my waiter asked me if I wanted gas. Well, normally I don't! But in restaurants all over Europe, Africa, and the Middle East they serve carbonated water with meals and they call it water "with gas." Regular water is 'still.'

2. Words change in meaning. It used to be that "crack" was something in the sidewalk, but now it is on the streets. CDs were financial investments. A fag used to be a cigarette, and smoking one made a lot of

people gay. A printer used to come home with ink on his hands. Oddly, if you call someone 'square' now, you are one. We are too polite today to say, "I'm going to the can (or John, or toilet)"; now we go to the 'bathroom' or the 'restroom' when most of them do not have baths nor is it the kind of place one would particularly care to rest. The fact that words change in meaning means that one must read older translations with caution.

For example, the King James Version says, "Suffer the little children to come unto me" (Matt 19:14). Once an elder was asked what this meant, and he said that we all must suffer a bit before we enter the kingdom of God. That is NOT what Jesus meant. In 1611 when the KJV was translated, 'suffer' meant "to allow or permit." That was four hundred years ago. Since the Bible was written over a period of 1400 years, some words, even within the Scriptures, change in meaning from earlier to later uses. For example, the Greek word *martyr* originally meant simply 'a witness' but by the time Revelation was written, enough of these Christian 'witnesses' had been killed for their faith that the word necessarily changed in meaning to incorporate this sacrifice of life for that which they affirmed.

3. English translations do not exactly or consistently represent the Greek and Hebrew word. Remember, the words we are defining in the Bible are not English. So we need to get back to the Greek and the Hebrew words (don't worry, we will show you how to do this in good time). Here is the problem: An English word such as 'love' will represent three different Greek words in the New Testament (*agape, phileo,* and *eros*). So if your goal is to learn what that particular *Greek* word is, you need to get behind each English translation and know what the Greek word is. Furthermore, each Greek word can be translated with multiple English words, so if you are intent on finding every New Testament use of a particular Greek word (and you should be, for that is the author's original language), then you will need to find all the places it is translated. The following chart will illustrate this:

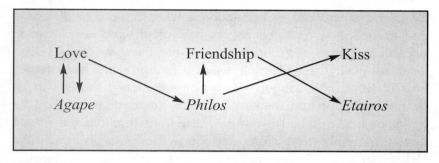

The English word love in the NIV is translated from two different Greek words: *agape* and *philos*. And while *agape* is always translated 'love,' *philos* is used for both 'friendship' and in the verb form 'kiss.' Then 'friendship' derives from both *philos* and *etairos*. This illustrates the complexity of translating a simple Greek word into English and then trying to find the definition of the Greek word based on the English translation. It is not an impossible task, but one does need to pay attention to both the English translation(s) and the Greek word(s) from which they come.

> *There is a really cool tool in the back of the NIV Concordance put out by Zondervan. It gives the Greek words (and how many times they are used) to translate each English word in the NIV (and vice versa). This is super helpful!*

4. Idioms. Every language has its own idioms. These nonliteral, often pictorial phrases make language all the more interesting. For instance, instead of saying, "Your actions are detrimental to my progress," one says, "You're killing me!" We have 'broken hearts' and 'pig-headed' friends. We are 'starving' because our waiter takes 'forever' at a restaurant. Our car is a 'lemon' and our new iPod is 'sweet.' These sorts of sayings are common in all languages. If you miss them in the original language of the Bible you probably won't miss much theologically, but you just won't smile as often. For example, reading through Jonah (4:2) in Hebrew, one discovers that God has a 'long nose.' What's that all about? Well, races with more swarthy skin cannot tell if a person is blushing with anger, so they watch the nose (in some cases in the Middle East persons have a rather considerable proboscis) to see if the nostrils flare. Flaring nostrils means your conversation partner is really upset. Hence, saying God has a long nose is a way of saying he is 'slow to anger.'

5. Transliterations. A translation is when a word or phrase in one language is replaced by an equivalent word or phrase in another language. A *transliteration* is when the same thing is done letter for letter. The end result is that a foreign word becomes an English word. The danger with a transliteration is that it can be given a definition from the new (receptor) language rather than the definition intended by the author. These transliterations are littered throughout Bible translations. Of course *Hallelujah* is simply the Hebrew phrase "Praise the Lord." No big deal there. Likewise, "Amen" means "let it be so." OK, no harm, no foul. However, what about the word 'deacon' (Greek *diakonos*)? In the original language it means 'servant,' specifically one who waits at a table. But in many churches a 'deacon' is a church official with voting rights. Or 'baptism' which meant 'to dunk or submerge' has been replaced by many for 'sprinkling.' Clearly some will want to argue just now about the theological correctness of these two positions. But this paragraph is not about theology but about linguistics. If there is a theologically valid point to the sprinkling or office of deacon (or twenty other words which could illustrate the point), then these should be made through context, not by an artificial transliteration of language that does not plainly give the meaning of the original. Watch for these transliterations and raise a red flag *every* time you meet them. Continue to ask, "Why was this not translated?" *and* "What difference in meaning does it make?"

6. Religious Terminology. Some words such as 'propitiation,' 'sanctification,' 'atonement,' 'saved,' 'sin,' etc. have meaning within Christianity that is more specific than its use in 'the world.' This is not surprising, for certain words are *always* appropriated by subcultures in idiosyncratic ways. (Computer geeks, for example, have their own language . . . it sounds like English, but it's clearly their own code!). We need to be careful with these words. Before racing to the Christian definition, we should first learn what the word meant in the broader culture and then narrow it down to how the church uses it. It might surprise you just how much more meaningful these words can become. For example 'redemption' was a fairly ordinary word in the slave trade. It was the price paid to purchase a slave. 'Redeemed' does not mean we were set free, and technically we were not! We were bought with a price that shifted our ownership from one master to another.

7. Words have sound when spoken. This might not mean much to those who read the Bible silently, but since the original texts were all read aloud in public, it was much more like a speech than a private devotional time. So if there was a play on words, a rhyme, or a repetition of sounds, it would add a bit of flavor to the reading of the word. Even if you can't hear the sounds yourself, your awareness of their presence will give you a greater appreciation of the sophistication and beauty of the Scriptures. Here are just four examples.

(1) An *alliteration* is "several sequential syllables starting with similar sounds" (get it?). Hebrews 1:1 is a pretty good example. Here is the transliteration of the Greek sentence; read it aloud for full phonetic effect: *"polumeros kai polutropos palai ho theos lalesas tois patrasin en tois prophetais."* That is just plain clever! However, because we don't read the Bible aloud in its original languages, these artistic devices are lost on us.

> *A good example*
> *of alliteration:*
> "Always assiduously
> avoid all alliterations."

(2) Assonance is when you repeat the same sound in several words in successive lines so that they have this kind of 'echo' effect. In other words, it is an extended rhyme. First Timothy 3:16 is a good example. The words 'vindicated,' 'seen,' 'preached,' 'believed,' and 'taken up' all end with the sound 'thay' in Greek. The effect is like a repetitious pounding of a drum that begs for a crescendo as Jesus ascends into heaven. One gets the impression that when this was read in the early church, the lector got louder and louder as he progressed through this poem.

(3) Paronomasia is a pun or a play on words. In Amos 8:2 there is a delightful little paronomasia that is completely lost in English. God asks Amos, "What do you see?" Amos replies, "A basket of ripe fruit." Then God said, "The end has come upon my people Israel; I will never again pass them by." Well, the imagery is powerful enough. But when you realize that 'ripe fruit' is *qayits* (קַיִץ) and 'end' is *qets* (קֵץ), the phrase is not only powerful but poetically beautiful. (Look carefully at the Hebrew words above and see just how close they are). Even when God passes a frightening judgment he is both artistic and clever.

(4) Onomatopoeia is when the word sounds like what it is (e.g., 'zip'). The old Batman and Robin comic books were famous

for this: 'Boom,' 'pow,' 'bam'! Once in a while you run into these in the Bible. Of course there will always be debate over onomatopoeia because we can't even agree if a dog says 'ruff' or 'whoof,' but here is one that is personally intriguing to me. In Genesis 1:2 it says the spirit 'hovered' over the water. The Hebrew word

> *Did you know . . .*
> *Approximately 85% of the ancient world was illiterate. So even when we are dealing with a written text, most people would still experience it orally.*

sounds something like *murachéfeth.* It almost sounds like the flutter of wings slapping against waves . . . but that could just be me.

The point is, reading the Bible is not just a cognitive experience. It can also be an oral one, and in the first-century world that was the norm. So we had better keep our ears open along with our eyes.

How Do You Define a Word?

At last we get to the meat of this chapter, and it is so simple it is almost embarrassing. There are only three sources for defining a word. (1) *One could look it up in the dictionary.* However, dictionaries, while convenient, are artificial and always dated. New words are being created, old ones are dying, and middle-aged words are putting on weight or going through a midlife crisis, even morphing into new forms. (2) So the best way to define a word is not in a book but on the street. *How are people actually using this word?* To what does it refer on MTV, CNN, Newsweek, and Google? Here is the axiom of defining a word: **a word means what the author uses it to mean**. Now this is not

> *Most words can mean several things but they cannot mean just anything.*

some arbitrary definition such as one finds in Alice in Wonderland's Tea Party. Rather, words and their definitions have social boundaries. If a word is to be used in a brand new way, there must be a social group large enough to adopt and implement this agreed-upon meaning. This sometimes happens through a charismatic leader (a rapper, a preacher, or a politician) whose followers use the word enough for it to become well-known. (All of us, I suppose, find ourselves quoting lines from a movie and having a friend finish it with us). Or it could arise from a technical guild such as medicine, fashion, economics, or sports. Even then, however, new word meanings are virtually always related to older, known definitions. For example, a computer chip is still a hard, flat little thing, just as a chip in your grandmother's porcelain tea pot, or a salty morsel which in England they call a 'crisp.' (3) Since words can mean several things, *one* **always** *must read in context* to determine how this particular word is being used in this particular instance.

Now, given these three sources for a word's definition—dictionary, common usage, and context—how does one relate these to biblical words which were originally in Greek and Hebrew? The answer is actually easier than you think. (1) Dictionary—look for dictionaries of Greek and Hebrew words [See Appendix B: Word Study Resources]. Here are three for non-Greek/Hebrew readers that will be very helpful. The simplest is *Strong's Concordance.* Each word has a number next to it (block numbers represent Hebrew, the italicized numbers represent Greek). In the back of this rather large book you can find these numbers and get a simple, one-sentence definition. *Vines Expository Dictionary of New Testament Words* gives longer definitions and combines synonymous words together. This is a *very* helpful book for English readers, but it

> For online use of the Strong's Concordance, *visit:* www.blueletterbible.org *or use* www.eliyah.com/lexicon.html. *For other great word study tools go to:* http://www.mybibletools.com/bible/word-study.htm.

is not comprehensive, so you won't be able to find every word. Far more complete, and far more technical is *The New International Dictionary of New Testament Theology.* It will cost you a pretty penny and you will seldom read the articles unless you are a Bible scholar or preacher. But one great advantage of this work is that it will not only give you the use of the word in the New Testament (it doesn't do Hebrew words), but it also traces the evolution of the word through Greek classical literature and the Greek Old Testament called the Septuagint (abbreviated 'LXX').

(2) Common Usage—Concordances list every use of every word in the entire Bible. They come in all shapes and sizes and for nearly every translation. But the best kind of concordance to get is one that runs on a computer. That way instead of just looking up

an individual word, you can look up phrases or several words at a time [using search criteria such as 'AND,' 'OR,' 'NOT'].

People often ask, "What is the best computer concordance out there?" My answer, *"The one you use!"* Look, a computer concordance is going to do virtually the same thing whether you pay $500 for the premier package (such as *Logos Software*) or whether you get a $15.95 special.[2] The important thing is that you are reading *every use* of the *Greek* or *Hebrew* word you are studying.

You can find the Logos Software at:
www.logos.com

This is far more important than even looking it up in a dictionary. After all, this is precisely how the editors of dictionaries come up with definitions. They look up the words in the original languages and just start reading verse after verse until they get a feel for the way(s) it is used. For contemporary words, there is no way to know how everyone is using the word (although GOOGLE helps), but for the Bible, the data pool has been pretty much the same for the last two millennia! Don't let some 'expert' tell you what a word means. Find out for yourself.

Now obviously Bible scholars and linguists can be incredibly helpful, but don't feel like you cannot know the meaning of a Bible word unless you read the original texts. That is simply no longer true. Furthermore, don't feel like you have to spend hundreds of dollars on books. Check out Appendix C, "Useful Websites for Bible Study." Here you can find thousands of dollars in books, commentaries, sermon preparation, devotional material, and classical sources. Don't get duped into buying a full featured package in a concordance when many of the works you buy are already free online and the others which are not online you will probably never use.

(3) Context—read your Bible! I mean it . . . read your Bible!!! This is the single most neglected practice in Bible study. We are prone to read all kinds of experts, trusting their opinions, rather than reading God's own message and trusting the guidance of the Holy Spirit. Please don't misunderstand: the Holy Spirit can also guide you through teachers, writers, counselors, and scholars, but the place to start and finish is in the Scriptures themselves.

---

[2] Better yet, go to http://www.discountchristian.com/freesoftware.html and order one for free!

Steps for Researching a Word

Now that you know the three sources for a word study, it is time to walk through a working guide for performing a word-study. These are not to be followed in mechanical precision, but for the first couple of times you research a biblical word, following these steps can assure you good results. [For dozens of examples of word studies by a master teacher, Kenny Boles, go to http://markmoore.org/classes/principles/wordstudies.html].

1. **Context**—read the sentence and paragraph in which your word is found. Get the general idea of the author's topic, mood, and argument.
2. **Translations**—Look up your passages in about five versions to see how your word is translated. Do all versions give the same word?
3. **Concordances**— *This is the core of your word study!* Spend most of your time here reading passages that actually use your word. As you do, try to categorize the uses of the words. Pretend that you have 3-5 manila folders (not more). Each verse must be slipped into one of the folders and labeled with a category that fits all the verses in the file. For example, if we were defining the word 'tree' in English we would find that it is used of a plant, a family genealogy, and an organizational chart. So these would be the three labels on our manila files and each usage we run across needs to fit into one of the folders. As you make your imaginary files, notice any clusters of words you find in the concordance. Is your word used a lot in a particular passage? By a particular author? In a particular genre? Within a particular covenant or time period? All of these may show a unique use of the word at a particular place and time.

   > For example, go to www.blueletterbible.org, and in the section entitled "Phrase Search/Concordance" type in the word "Wisdom" and press enter. The page that opens will give all of the times in which the word is used at the bottom of the page. As you examine, notice the significant cluster of "wisdom" in the book of Job. Are there other books in which "wisdom" occurs at a high frequency?

4. **Etymology**—This refers to the 'family history' of a word. Often words are derived from other words. For example,

'understand' is made up of 'under' and 'stand.' In addition, some English words are based on Greek words such as 'dynamite' which comes from the Greek word *dynamis* meaning 'power.' Etymology is not a primary consideration for you, but if you run across a word with an interesting family history (etymology), it will make your reading (and teaching) more interesting. This is kind of like talking to a relative of yours and finding out that you are related to Abraham Lincoln or Mussolini or someone else (in)famous.

5. **Nonbiblical usage**—This is very hard to get at if you only know English. But *The New International Dictionary of New Testament Theology*, as well as many of the finer commentaries will point out how a word was used in secular Greek before it ever made it into the Bible. Some of these background studies can open up the meaning of a word in its biblical use. So if someone cites some obscure Greek poet or Roman historian, stop for a moment and take a closer look to see how this word was used outside the Scriptures. This is not likely the kind of thing you will notice on your own (props to you if you do!). But now that you know to look for it, you will consistently read in commentaries how scholars describe the uses of words outside the Bible. By the way, the Perseus Project has now made locating and searching classical sources available to the common person without a huge library—it's all online at: http://www.perseus.tufts.edu/.

6. **Synonyms/Antonyms**—Many words have brothers and sisters. Words that say pretty much the same thing (synonyms) and those that say almost the opposite (antonyms) will allow you to see the family portrait rather than an individual photo. Words are sometimes defined by comparison to similar words or opposite words as well as by their own usages. This is particularly true when your word is used in a list. Pay special attention when your word comes in pairs or sets.

7. **Dictionaries and Word Studies**—Only *after* you have looked up every usage of your word and put them into cat-

egories should you refer to dictionaries and word studies performed by other scholars. They will invariably sharpen your own thinking. But if you look to them first, you will be biased toward their reading rather than doing your own thinking. This is not to say that you are smarter than experts in the field. However, your

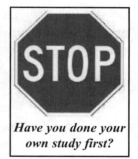

Have you done your own study first?

own discoveries will be more meaningful than second-hand sources. Let the Bible speak to you first, then let God use the words of others' research to speak to you as well. Now, let me add here that I personally believe that hermeneutics must be a community project; it certainly was in the early church. That is, we read and discuss texts together and in light of the community wisdom, both past and present, we apply ancient texts to modern contexts. However, all your life you have been listening and absorbing. If you are to genuinely contribute to the dialogue, it is important for you to develop independent thinking. Don't ever let this become isolated thinking, but for now, start your Bible study with your own research rather than immediately relying on others.

8. **Commentaries**—Any substantive commentary will help with major word studies. After doing your own research, read two or three commentaries on your text and see what they have to say about your particular word.

9. **Context**—When all is said and done, go back to where you started. Read the passage again (and again) and decide which of the manila folders your word belongs in.

Rules for Interpreting Words

The following ten rules are the bare essentials when doing a word study. They describe, in briefest fashion, how words work. Please post these as boundary markers in your mind for the parameters of your own word studies. Listening to the online lecture (Words: Parts 1–5) for this entire chapter would be beneficial

since much of this compact
writing is unpacked in the
audio format.

To download any of Mark's lectures go to: www.markmoore.org/resources/lectures.html

1. Every word has only one intended meaning in each use—the author's (barring, of course, puns and other figures of speech). Therefore, context and usage determine the definition of a word. The best way to determine the meaning of a word is to play mental "follow the leader with the author."
2. Words have multiple meanings within a given range. They also change, grow, get married, have kids, and sometimes die.
3. Meaning is not found in words, or even in sentences, but in the pericope.
4. Law of Parsimony: All other factors being equal, the simplest explanation is to be preferred. When in doubt, trust the generic or traditional definition. The Holy Spirit is more likely to work in a godly group of educated translators than in your own individual novelty.
5. Every word is interchangeable with its meaning. In other words, if you can plug your definition of the word into the sentence and read the biblical author's sentence smoothly and with clarity, you have a good definition.
6. Clusters of a word in one passage may offer a good definition for the word.
7. Words are to be understood literally unless the context demands otherwise, and this would include religious and technical terminology. While every language and every speaker uses figures of speech and metaphoric language, this is not the place to start. Only where the literal definition creates a tension, contradiction, or nonsensical construction should one revert to nonliteral understandings of words.
8. New or rare words are defined first by context, then etymology, the earliest versions, and finally by kindred languages and analogous words. (This is a rare complexity you probably won't have to worry with unless your word is used less than five times in the whole Bible).
9. Most NT authors are Hebraic in thought, therefore one may need to trace the word back to the OT. This point has

already been made in our chapter on history, but it bears repeating here. Looking at the Greek word alone may not be enough. You see, for most of the authors of the NT (Luke excepted), Aramaic (a cousin language of Hebrew) was their first language and the OT was their Bible. Hence, it is *always* appropriate, and often necessary, to see how a word was used in its OT background.

10. Synonyms, when used together, generally accentuate their similarity rather than their differences unless a particularly acute distinction is being made. This is especially true in poetry.

Summary

Words are the building blocks of language and an indispensable part of any study of Scripture. The bad news is that word studies are complex, sometimes baffling. The good news is that by following the exercises designed below, you can actually research the meaning of Greek and Hebrew words without actually knowing those languages. Through the use of computer concordances, you can do study that a generation ago was limited to the scholarly towers of seminary. Be patient with yourself as you learn this new skill. It takes time, sometimes a bit of coaching, but the end result is a new awareness of the rich fullness of biblical language. That will make all your efforts worth the time and energy invested.

Going Further:

Assignments and Further Reading

Assignment #7:

✍ In this assignment, we are going to be selecting the words that we will use in our word studies. So first, make a photocopy of your text, or print it off of the internet from: http://www.blueletterbible.org (this website will be vital for the following assignments).

✍ On the copy of your passage, circle 3-5 words for major word studies. There are several key elements to look for when trying to determine which words are important for major word studies. (1) Look for words that seem to be pivotal for the meaning of your passage. (2) Look for words repeated in your text. (3) Look for theologically loaded words. (4) Look for perplexing or unclear words and figures of speech. These guidelines will lead you to the major words of your passage to study in more depth.

✍ Finally, underline 5-10 words for minor word studies. As you are trying to establish which words to use as major word studies you will inevitably run across other words that seem important but not necessarily crucial. These are the words on which you will want to do minor word studies. Often, in the course of your study, you will drop a major one to a minor or raise a minor to a major; this is to be expected.

Assignment #8:

✍ The purpose of this assignment is to get you acquainted with the Blue Letter Bible online search tool (found at: http://www.blueletterbible.org/). You will need to have access to the internet while you are going through this assignment as it will lead you through various exercises utilizing the features that the Blue Letter Bible offers for you, which you will want to become familiar with in order to do the following assignments.

1. Go to: http://www.blueletterbible.org/.
2. As you can tell from the opening page, this website offers an incredible amount of information and study tools to the patient student who is willing to search throughout the website to utilize its resources. For our purposes, however, let's look for information about a specific word.

   a. At the top of the page, there is a box that is labeled "New Bible Search." In this box, type in "Acts 2:38" and press enter.

   b. To the left of the verse written in the KJV, you will notice a cluster of 6 boxes labeled "K," "C," "L," "I," "V," and "D," respectively [Note: sometimes the "I" box will be replaced with a musical staff if there are hymns available that correlate with the particular text you are studying]. In order, the boxes are linked to: Treasury of **K**nowledge, **C**oncordance and Hebrew/Greek, **L**ist of Available Commentaries, **I**mages and Maps, **V**ersions/Translations, and **D**ictionary Aids.

   c. For our purposes, select the "C" to open the Concordance and Hebrew/Greek study tool for Acts 2:38. When the page reloads, the verse you have selected will be broken down into several categories that are linked with various tools to study the words or phrases in more depth. Next to "be baptized," click on the Strong's number [907]. When the page reloads, answer the question: How many times is this word used in the KJV? _____

   d. For your convenience, scroll down to the bottom of this page to read every time that this word is used in the Bible in its written context. Read through these verses at your leisure to get a feel for how this word is used.

3. Let's do another search for the word 'baptism.'
   a. Either repeat steps 1-2a above, or you can simply press the "back" arrow on your internet browser 2 times to go back to Acts 2:38 with the available tools listed in the 6 boxes to the left of the text.
   b. Once you are back to Acts 2:38, click on the box marked "D" on the left. The screen will reopen with a drop-down box below Acts 2:38 labeled: "Choose Dictionary Topic for Acts 2:38—Then Click Go."
   c. Click on the drop-box and go to the *Naves Topical Bible*. Click on the first entry on Baptism, which is labeled "Baptism—Christian."
   d. The following page will have Scripture references broken up into three separate categories "John's," "Christian," and "Of The Holy Spirit." As you might have guessed, these are all the cross-references for the topic of baptism. To read each of these passages in its context, simply click on the hyperlinks and the Blue Letter Bible will take you to the chosen text. This will be invaluable for you when you are looking up parallel passages for your selected text.
4. If you wanted to compare your text in various translations, the Blue Letter Bible conveniently allows you to do this with relative ease.
   a. From the *Nave's Topical Bible* page either click the "back" arrow on your internet browser 1 time to go back to Acts 2:38 with the available tools listed in the 6 boxes to the left of the text, or you can repeat steps 1-2a above.
   b. When you are back to Acts 2:38, click on the box marked "V" on the left. The screen will reopen with 13 different translations opened up in parallel form (the translations include: KJV, NKJV, NLT, NIV, ESV, NASB, RSV, ASV, Young's Literal Translation, Darby's Translation, Noah Webster's Translation, HNV, and Jerome's Latin Vulgate).

c. Reading through the parallel translations can clue you in to various difficulties or variants found in the text.

5. Spend 15 more minutes just tinkering to see what you can find on your own text.

6. Obviously it is easy to get lost in this program. Don't worry about it. You won't break it! But a few minutes of sleuthing will save you hours of turning pages in your Bible.

Assignment #9:

✍ Go to http://www.blueletterbible.org/. In the appropriate box, type in the text where the word for your first major word study appears. To the left of the text, click on the "C" button to take you to a Greek/English concordance that also includes Strong's number reference. Using this feature of the Blue Letter Bible, answer the following questions.

1. Choose one of your major words to study and write it here: _____

2. How many times is that word used in the Bible? _____

3. What other derivatives of that word are used? (For example the word "faith" is also found as "faithful," "faithfully," "faithless," etc.) Write down all the derivatives.

4. What Hebrew and Greek words are used to translate your major word? Write the words as well as the Goodrich/ Kohlenberger number used to identify it (or the Strong's number).
Hebrew: Greek:

5. Which of the Hebrew or Greek words above is used in your passage?   _____

6. Look up that particular Hebrew or Greek word and tell what other English words are used to translate it in the

NIV and how many times it is translated by each of these words.

7. How many times is your Greek or Hebrew word used in the Bible? _____

8. Which book is it found in most? _____

9. Identify any significant clusters of this word by author, covenant or genre:

10. What is the Strong's number assigned to your particular Hebrew or Greek word? _____

11. Using a Greek dictionary in the back of a Strong's concordance (or any other Greek dictionary available to you), give a one- to two-sentence definition of your word.

12. Briefly describe the difference in how Young's concordance lists words and the NIV.

✍ These questions will give you a great synopsis of your particular major word and how it is used in the text you are studying. Make sure you have taken the time to answer each one as thoroughly as possible.

Assignment #10:

✍ Choose a second word on which you will do another major word study. While the following process varies from the previous assignment, you will discover some significant parallels in the procedure.

1. Find your passage at: http://www.blueletterbible.org/. To refresh your memory, follow step 2a from *Assignment #8.*

   ♦ Click on the "C" button to the left of your passage to pull up the concordance break-down of your passage.

   ♦ Next, click on the Strong's Number to pull up the lexicon results for your particular word.

2. Using the lexicon results page from above, write below the following information about the word you are researching:

   ♦ English Word: _____

♦ Transliteration: _____ (This will be found under the section entitled "Pronunciation Guide").

3. On the same lexicon results page, go to the section entitled "Thayer's Lexicon *(Help)*." If applicable, click the hyperlink at the bottom of the section labeled "(MORE)." With the entire entry in "Thayer's Lexicon" expanded, read the entry describing the various definitions for the word you are studying.

4. Now, write out a brief definition of your word.

5. Write here any synonyms, cognates, or Hebrew equivalents given in "Thayer's Lexicon" in the section entitled "[SYN . . .]."

6. Scroll down the page until you come to the list of Scripture references in which your word is found. Using this section, answer the following questions.

7. How many times is your word used? _____

8. By which author(s) is it used and how many times each?

_____

_____

_____

_____

9. In what book(s) is it used most? _____

10. Either press the "back" arrow on your internet browser 2 times to go back to your text, or repeat steps 1-2a on *Assignment #8*.

   ♦ Click on the "V" button found on the left side of your text. This will bring up the list of 13 versions/translations for your text.

   ♦ Using this list of translations, answer the following question:

11. How many different words are used to translate it and how many times each? _____

_____

_____

_____

12. Finally, click the "L" button to the left of your passage. On the new page, a drop-down box will appear

under your text which will read "Please Choose a Commentary for [your text] — Then Click 'Go.'"

♦ From this drop-down box, choose three commentaries on your particular passage and read them thoroughly.

♦ Jot down any significant grammatical observations that may prove to be important for your text and for your word in particular.

✍ This exercise will force you to utilize all of the resources found on the Blue Letter Bible in order to determine the meaning of your particular word. At any time, feel free to substitute another resource with which you are more comfortable. While the Blue Letter Bible is an easily accessible resource with loads of possibilities, the goal is for you to simply understand your word and your passage more fully.

Assignment #11:

✍ In this exercise, you are going to make a translation chart for the words on which you are doing major and minor word studies. You will want to compile a minimum of 5 versions/translations in your chart, but use more if possible.

✍ Find your passage at: http://www.blueletterbible.org/. To refresh your memory, follow step 2a from *Assignment #8*.

♦ Click on the "V" button found on the left side of your text. This will bring up the list of 13 versions/translations for your text.

♦ Make a chart by either copying these texts into Microsoft Word in a chart form, or simply write each of the translations out paralleling them line by line.

✍ The purpose of this exercise is to compare the various translations to see how various people have translated the original Greek or Hebrew into English. Often times, significant variations between translations can be key clues to difficulties or theological issues in the text.

Assignment #12:

✍ Now you are ready. Choose another one of your words to do a major word study on from your text. Use Blue Letter Bible to do all of the necessary procedures to identify the range of meaning for your particular word. Then, underline the single sentence that most clearly defines your word as used in the context of the passage. After doing your own word study, read three of the short word studies done by Kenny Boles at http://markmoore.org/classes/principles/wordstudies.html.

See Appendixes B and C for helpful resources for word studies.

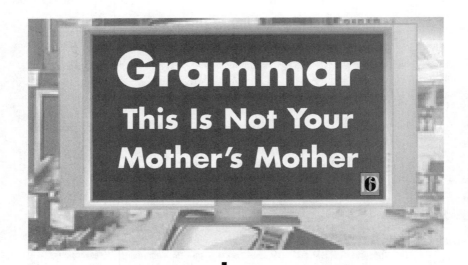

Grammar
This Is Not Your Mother's Mother

6

Lincoln Logs, Erector Sets, and Legos are seductive even when we're grown because we just love building stuff! More fun than building stuff, however, is tearing it apart to see how it works. If something breaks in my house, it is surprising the speed at which an electric screw driver mysteriously appears in my hand and begs for implementation! Often these broken devices prove to be irreparable (meaning I can't figure out how to put it back together). Or, just as often they do actually get reassembled but with vestigial parts left over on my work bench.

Since so many of us resonate with this primal drive to deconstruction, it seems rather odd that so many of these same people have such an aversion to grammar. Perhaps this is due to some successful secret conspiracy of evil English teachers who plotted to make our lives miserable. We were forced to learn terms like 'nominal suffix' and 'prepositional phrases' and then plot them on a graph called 'a line diagram.' Well, if you hated that kind of grammar, you are in luck here. Even if we were inclined to guide you through that kind of grammar, what good would it do since it would have to be in Hebrew, Aramaic, and Greek? Don't get the idea that these are uninteresting. For a few of us linguistic mutants they are eminently fascinating (if you've never experienced a good 'pluperfect,' you just don't know what you're missing). We simply have to face the fact that we are English readers of the Bible, and we must do what we can with what we have.

Fortunately, grammar is not the most important element of interpretation. There are times that grammar makes a huge difference. Story time: There was this little kid named Johnny who hated grammar and gave his English teacher fits. One day, in fact, he was so bad that the teacher made him stay after school to teach him a lesson. She wrote on the board "Johnny said the teacher is an idiot." She then asked little Johnny if he agreed with the sentence. He defiantly nodded his head and said, "Yes, I agree!" To his utter amazement the teacher said, "I agree with it too." She then turned around and punctuated the sentence as follows: "Johnny," said the teacher, "is an idiot!" Seldom does grammar make such a significant difference, but sometimes, even in the Bible it does.

For example, the NIV punctuates Romans 9:5 this way: "Theirs [of the Jews] are the patriarchs, and from them is traced the human ancestry of Christ, who is God over all, forever praised! Amen." This is a clear declaration that Jesus is God, right? Not according to the punctuation of the RSV. It says, "To them [to the Jews] belong the patriarchs, and of their race, according to the flesh, is the Christ. God who is over all be blessed for ever. Amen." Oh my, what a difference a simple period can make! There are other places where grammar is significant as well. Look at Acts 23:8. It says: "The Sadducees say that there is no resurrection, and that

> *Did you know that in the original Old Testament there was no punctuation? In fact, there were not even any vowels. Both were added after the time of Jesus by Jewish scribes called 'Massoretes.' How is this possible? Well, can you read this? JCK WNT T TH MLL. (Hint: it is missing two 'a's, two 'e's, and one 'o.' Even if you wonder whether the last word has an 'i" rather than an 'a,' reading it in context could probably tell you the answer.)*

there are neither angels nor spirits, but the Pharisees acknowledge them all." Strictly speaking, that is not true; after all, the Sadducees were firm believers in the Torah (that is, the first five books of the Old Testament). There were certainly angels and spirits there, so why would they not believe in them? Actually, what they rejected was the idea that a human being could resurrect as an angel or as a spirit. A simple change of punctuation would make this clear: "The Sadducees say that there is no resurrection: neither angels nor spirits." That is, one cannot resurrect as either an angel or some other kind of spirit.

 *This is a picture of a Hebrew text without vowels or punctuation. Compare the first and third letters highlighted. One has no space between the left leg of the letter and the top bar; the other does. This portion of the letter was called the 'tittle.' The second highlighted letter 'yot' (or 'jot') is the smallest letter of the Hebrew alphabet. Jesus promised that not even these smallest portions of the law would pass away (Matt 5:18).*

So far all we have looked at is punctuation. Strictly speaking, however, grammar is about the placement of the words more than how they are marked. In English, for example, we say, "The big, white, lovely mansion." So you don't really know what is big, white, and lovely until the end of the sentence. In Spanish, however, it makes more sense—the word 'mansion' goes right up front and all the descriptors follow. In English we all know that sentences are formed by subject, verb, object. Not so in Hebrew which tends to put verbs up front.

> *Meaning of words (lexicography), form and function of words (morphology), and order of words (syntax) make up the whole of grammar.*

Speaking of Hebrew verbs, they are very cool. There is virtually no past, present, or future tense of verbs (of course they had ways of expressing time, but not by the verbs themselves). However, they had seven different kinds of verbal actions. Let's illustrate with the word 'kiss.' In Hebrew, one could simply kiss (1) or simply be kissed (2). Or one could kiss intensely (3) or be kissed intensely (4). Or one could cause to kiss (5) or cause to be kissed (6).[1] Or you could kiss

---

[1] How, you might ask is that possible to cause someone else to kiss? A preacher does it when he pronounces a couple husband and wife. There are other ways too. It is time for an irrelevant story: We were on a campus visit at a Bible College where this kid planned to attend the following year as a freshman. A woman walked out of the cafeteria and I dared this kid to run up and kiss her on the cheek for a dollar. So being young and dumb, he did. But what I knew that he did not know was that this woman was the college president's wife. What a way to start your college career!

yourself (7), a far more difficult task one would think, though the lipstick on the mirrors in girls' Jr. High bathrooms indicate that it is, in fact, a notable desire. [Actually a better illustration for this last action would be 'untying yourself'—it is an action you both do and receive at the same time.] However, as we mentioned before, much of this is beyond the average English reader. So what can we do to better understand the grammar of the Bible just by reading English?

Diagrammatical Analysis

Now there's a great-big hairy term—'diagrammatical analysis.' However, it is really quite simple. All we're going to do is take the words from the Bible and structure them in such a way that we can see the syntactical relationships of the sentences. Simply put, we are going to make a picture from the words themselves that show the most important thoughts of the pericope and how the main ideas relate to one another. If we do this right, an outline for a sermon or lesson will emerge from the text itself rather than an artificial structure being imposed on the text. Here's the plan, first take a look at the couple of samples on the next two pages and see if you can figure out what is going on. Then we will offer you five simple steps to follow in order to produce your own on the text you are studying.

Simple Guidelines for a Diagrammatical

1. **Import** the biblical text into a word processor. After you have your text in a separate document, put each thought from the text on a separate line (using your <Enter> key to break up sentences). Don't be afraid to break up sentences into single phrases or even smaller units, just so long as each individual thought is on its own line. Now that you have the text all in one block, with each idea at the left margin, we can start working through it.

2. **Indent** everything except the main ideas. Read through your passage three or four times and try to determine the most important ideas. Indent everything else one

> *A diagrammatical tends to work best with epistles. It is sometimes less helpful with prophecy and narrative. With poetry it can be downright tough.*

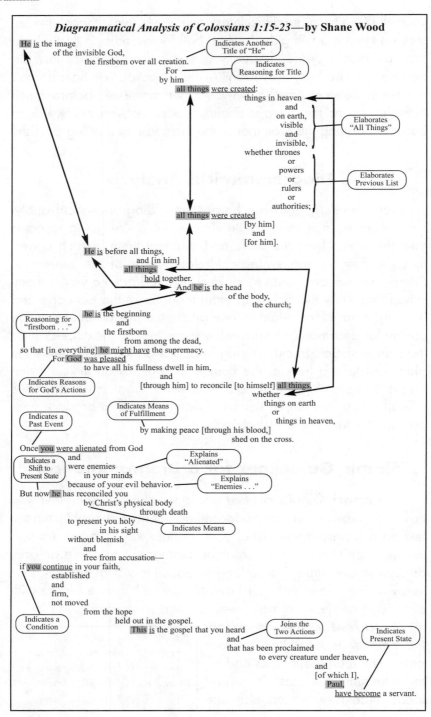

Diagrammatical Analysis of Colossians 1:15-23—by Shane Wood

Diagrammatical Analysis of John 7:53–8:11—By Brianna Zwart

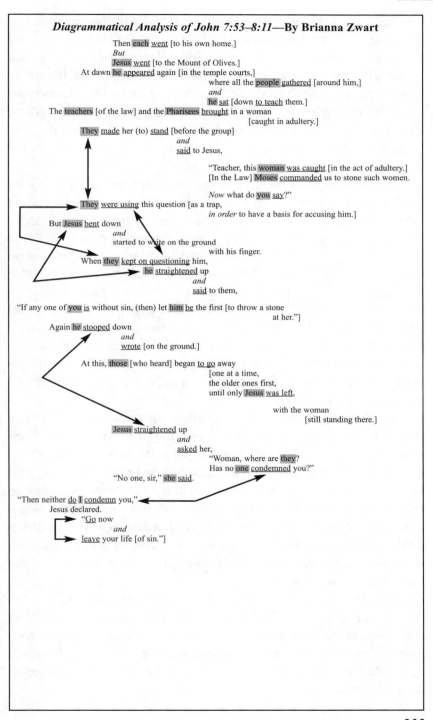

Then each went [to his own home.]
But
Jesus went [to the Mount of Olives.]
At dawn he appeared again [in the temple courts,]
where all the people gathered [around him,]
and
he sat [down to teach them.]
The teachers [of the law] and the Pharisees brought in a woman
[caught in adultery.]
They made her (to) stand [before the group]
and
said to Jesus,

"Teacher, this woman was caught [in the act of adultery.]
[In the Law] Moses commanded us to stone such women.

Now what do you say?"

They were using this question [as a trap,
in order to have a basis for accusing him.]

But Jesus bent down
and
started to write on the ground
with his finger.

When they kept on questioning him,
he straightened up
and
said to them,

"If any one of you is without sin, (then) let him be the first [to throw a stone
at her."]

Again he stooped down
and
wrote [on the ground.]

At this, those [who heard] began to go away
[one at a time,
the older ones first,
until only Jesus was left,

with the woman
[still standing there.]

Jesus straightened up
and
asked her,
"Woman, where are they?
Has no one condemned you?"
"No one, sir," she said.

"Then neither do I condemn you,"
Jesus declared.
"Go now
and
leave your life [of sin."]

111

tab stop. It might help if you first indent all but five or six lines. Now look only at those important ideas and decide what you will keep at the left and what you will indent. Let me be clear: You are leaving the most important ideas on the left margin and indenting everything else one "tab stop." **The fewer lines you leave on the left margin the better your diagram will be.** Work at this until you have only **one to three** lines at the left margin. Sometimes this main idea will be right up front, sometimes at the very end, and sometimes in the middle.

Further indent everything except the secondary ideas. Once you've got the main ideas (1-3) at the left margin, try to decide what are the second most important ideas (perhaps 2-4 under each main idea). Leave them indented one

CAUTION:
There is no one right way to do a diagrammatical analysis.

"tab stop" and indent everything else another "tab stop." Your text should begin to look like a mountain range turned on its side. Continue this step with the third most important ideas, then fourth, then fifth. There is no specific guideline as to how far you can indent something. Much of this is subjective interpretation, but the core of it, done correctly, will reveal (1) the main ideas of the passage and (2) clarify the important syntactical relationships.

4. **Arrange** *dependent clauses (prepositional phrases, adverbial phrases, and relative clauses) in one of two ways.* They can either go on a separate line directly underneath the word they modify or they can stay on the same line but put inside a square bracket to show it is a separate idea. You might have two or three dependent clauses that 'hang together' in this way. Again, there is no one right way to do this. The point of this exercise is not scientific precision so that yours looks like everyone else's. The point is to draw a picture by visually showing the connections and relationships of the passage.

Arrange connectives ('and,' 'but,' 'therefore,' 'in addition to,' etc.) in the same way. They can go in the sentence in brackets or on a line all by themselves. However, the very nature of connectives is that they connect two separate ideas. Therefore, they will not likely be in brackets in the middle of the line but at the beginning of a new line.

*5. **Mark** up your diagrammatical to show special relationships.* This will be done in three ways. First, and most importantly, identify the subject and main verb of each sentence—highlight the subject (or **bold**) and underline the main verb of each sentence. Second [and less frequently], draw a line between two related items if there is a parallelism or a chiasm in the paragraph. This is particularly helpful to show connections or structures that span several sentences. Third [and not always necessary], in a separate comment box, put into your own words what you notice is happening with the structure of the text.

This simple exercise of identifying, in English, the subject, main verb, and conjunctions of a sentence can yield great insight. Here is an important example of each:

Example #1: Romans 8:26, "We do not know what we ought to pray for, but the Spirit himself intercedes for us with groans that words cannot express." In the first phrase, 'we' is the subject and the verb is 'do not know.' In the second phrase, 'Spirit' is the subject and 'intercedes' is the main verb. Both phrases are separated by the simple conjunction 'but,' indicating a contrast between the two parts of the sentence. Interpretation: We are ignorant BUT the Spirit intercedes. Now, some Christians use this verse to justify speaking in tongues. Don't misunderstand, this is not a criticism of speaking in tongues. It is however a criticism of using this verse to justify doing so, especially with unintelligible language. You see, it is not we who groan (we, in fact, are ignorant at this point). Rather, the Spirit communicates clearly for us, not with language at all, but with groans that surpass language.

Example #2: Hebrews 12:1, "Therefore, since we are surrounded by such a great cloud of witnesses, let us throw off everything that hinders and the sin that so easily entangles, and let us run with perseverance the race marked out for us." Question: Who are these witnesses? Well, look at the first conjunction of this sentence, 'therefore.' This word indicates a conclusion based on a previous narrative. The chapter division at this point is entirely misleading. You will never understand the witnesses of 12:1 until you connect it with the 'Hall of Fame of the Faith' in chapter 11! These witnesses are not heavenly angels looking down on our terrestrial contest. These are the other athletes who have run before us and now line the track cheering us on to finish what they started. In the end, they are not looking at us so much as we are to look to them to run after their example.

Conclusion

And there you have it, a simple exercise (once you've done it a couple of times), that will allow you as an English-only reader, to see the grammatical structure of the text in a nontechnical way. Let's conclude with two important principles concerning grammar and Bible study. First, recognize that you don't know enough to analyze a Greek or Hebrew passage. That's OK, it's not the most important part of Bible study. However, it should also tell you to pay attention to scholars who do know what they are talking about. Don't blow off grammatical observations in commentaries! You can't afford to ignore grammar just because it is unpleasant for you. Second, the study of grammar won't solve all the problems of difficult passages, but it will narrow the range of possibilities. For example, 1 Corinthians 13:10, speaking of the gift of tongues, prophecy, and knowledge, says that when the 'perfect' comes, the partial will be done away. So at some point in time these gifts will pass away. When? Well, when the 'perfect' comes. What is the perfect? Jesus, right? Wrong! The word 'perfect' is in the neuter gender, not the masculine. Therefore, the 'perfect' could be the end of time, it could be the completion of the canon of Scriptures, it could be the maturity of the church, but the 'perfect' cannot be, grammatically speaking, Jesus himself.

> There are three important tools that will help
> English-only readers identify grammar:
> (1) Compare various **translations** of the Bible.
> (2) A Greek/English **interlinear** will help you see
> the original construction of the sentence.
> (http://www.studylight.org/isb/).
> (3) A good (or at least a thick) Bible **commentary**.

Grammar may not be the most interesting part of your study of the Bible. Nonetheless, God was courteous enough to give us language and then communicate with us through that medium. The least we can do is pay attention, and the easiest way we know of doing that is through this simple diagrammatical analysis. Through this exercise you allow the text to reveal its own structure and relationship rather than picking and choosing from that text what you personally find interesting or significant.

Going Further:

Assignments and Further Reading

Assignment #13:

✍ Using your passage, make a transitional word chart following the example found below.

Example of a Transitional Word Chart
Based on 1 Timothy 4:6-10 (NASV)

Verse & Transitional Word	Usual Function	Significance
6. And (*kai*)	Connective of series or addition	Connects the two things that Timothy is supposed to nourish himself on: words of faith and sound doctrine.
7. But (*de*) Another and (*kai*) is evident in Greek	Connectives of contrast. Probably force is fairly strong here.	Contrasts what Timothy is to nourish himself on and what he is to avoid—worldly fables.
7. On the other hand (*de*)	Connectives of contrast. Probably strong here.	In contrast to worldly fables is Paul's command to discipline self for godliness.
8. For (*gar*)	Connective of reason.	States the reason why Timothy is to discipline himself: it profits some.
8. But (*de*)	Connective of contrast	Contrasts bodily discipline and godliness. Godliness is profitable for all things.
8. Since (not in Greek)	Connective of result or concession. Sometimes shows purpose.	Paul shows how godliness is profitable for all things.
8. And also (*nun kai*)	Connective of series or addition	Connects present life with life to come.
10. For (*gar*)	Connective of reason. May not have the full force here	The reason the statement is trustworthy is because men give their labor for it.
10. Because (*hoti*)	Connective of reason. Can introduce quote. Can this be the statement of v. 10?	States reason that we labor and strive, or it is the content of the faithful saying: God saves believers.

Assignment #14:

✍ Using your text, make a mechanical layout/diagrammatical analysis, following the steps outlined in this chapter. At the bottom of the page, in a sentence or two, explain how this pericope is connected to the one before and the one following it. This will remind you through this detailed exegetical exercise that the context of the passage is vital in determining your text's A.I.M.

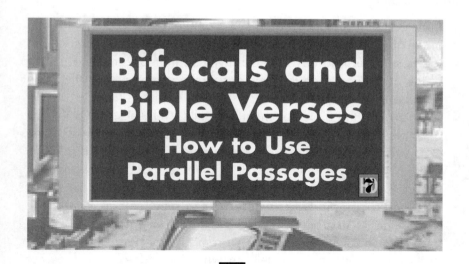

Bifocals and Bible Verses
How to Use Parallel Passages

The use of parallel passages in Bible study is kind of like bifocals. The dual lens allows you to see both close-up and far away. In a similar fashion, by keeping one eye on the horizon and the other on the text in your hands you are able to see the whole biblical landscape more clearly. Or perhaps using an auditory metaphor, it is more fun to listen to music in stereo than mono. You get a sense of the richness of the music and the fullness of the composition that just can't come through a single speaker. This is what it is like to listen to parallel passages. You can see the same topic but from different angles and hear the same teaching in stereo.

This assumes, of course, that while the Bible is a collection of sixty-six books, they are all ultimately from one God. That is, the Bible is a unified whole. If you don't happen to believe the

---

Focal Fun-Facts

- *A.D. 1280 = The first corrective lenses were made in Florence, Italy, by Allessandro della Spina, a Dominican Friar. They were made for Salvino degli Armati, a physicist, whose eyes were damaged during light refraction experiments. These first glasses utilized convex lenses to correct the farsightedness of Armati.*
- *A.D. 14th century = The first concave lenses were used to correct nearsightedness. The exact creator and first user are unknown.*
- *A.D. 1760 = Benjamin Franklin is credited with the invention of bifocals (both concave and convex lenses in the same frames) in 1760.*

Bible comes from God, then placing one text next to another might make no more sense than harmonizing Gandhi with Churchill. But for those of us who have been convinced that God is the architect of the Scriptures, then the best and first commentary on the Bible must be the Bible itself.

How can the Bible comment on itself? Well, let's take a look at a simple example. John 15:16 says, ". . . **the Father will give you whatever you ask in my name**." FAR OUT!!! This is better than an episode of *I Dream of Jeannie*. Let's see, I want a Jaguar (the car), a career as a famous musician, a smokin' hot wife, 2.5 kids, and a big, big house where we can play football. Is that really what this verse promises? Well, a few parallel passages might just put some parameters around this promise. Pay particular attention to the bold print and you tell me what Jesus does and does not promise through the following passages: "**If you believe**, you will receive whatever you ask for in prayer" (Matt 21:22). "I will do whatever you ask **in my name**, so that the Son may bring glory to the Father" (John 14:13). "**If you remain in me and my words remain in you**, ask whatever you wish, and it will be given you" (John 15:7). "When you ask, you do not receive, because **you ask with wrong motives**, that you may spend what you get on your pleasures" (Jas 4:3). "We have confidence before God and receive from him anything we ask, **because we obey his commands** and do what pleases him" (1 John 3:21b-22). "This is the confidence we have in approaching God: that if we ask anything **according to his will**, he hears us. And if we know that he hears us—whatever we ask—we know that we have what we asked of him," (1 John 5:14-15).

It should be obvious that the promise of John 15:16 is not *carte blanche* for spoiled brats. It is a promise from our commander-in-chief that, when we carry out his commission, he will support us in every necessary way to accomplish his will in this world. This is but one example of how parallel passages can open up meaning of a text. Or perhaps it would be better to say that it is an example of how parallel passages 'constrain' the meaning of a text and keep interpreters from going hog wild with proof-texts.

Think of it this way: when we live in real relationships, there is seldom a closed conversation. That is, families often continue to dialogue about work, morals, politics, and fair play. There is not *the* talk about the birds and the bees, for example. Rather, most parents have multiple discussions through the course of raising their children. The conversation with a four-year-old about the importance of keeping his pants on at preschool should differ significantly from a conversation with a sixteen-year-old going out on her first date (though the advice may still be the same). Likewise, parallel passages allow us to trace the conversations that God had with his people through the development of sacred history. We pick up various snippets along the way. Where we have the opportunity to hear the whole conversation, by all means, we should take it.

Types of Parallels

Parallelism is not like a mathematical equation: X + Y = Z. Rather, parallels come in shades. There are lots of different shades of blue and some of them are much closer on the palette than others. While identifying these shades is not exactly an exact science, no one denies that some outfits match while others clash. Parallels are kind of like that—some are more closely 'shaded' in meaning or vocabulary than others. So let your inner artist come out for a bit while we discuss the various ways of 'color-matching' biblical parallels.

> *Two Types of Parallels*
>
> Some parallels are **verbal**: *the author uses the exact words of another or at least words close enough to recognize the allusion or common source. Other parallels are **topical**: they talk about the same subject, but their vocabulary is very different.*

(1) **Synoptic Parallels**—The word 'synoptic' comes from two Greek words meaning 'seen' and 'together.' It refers most often to Matthew, Mark, and Luke, since these three overlap quite a bit in the stories they tell. The 'shades' here are almost exactly the same. You frequently find the same words or the same descriptions in these books. However, the Synoptic Gospels are not the only books in the Bible with substantial verbal overlap. First and Second Samuel along with 1 and 2 Kings are retold in the books of 1 and 2 Chronicles. It is really interesting to read them carefully side by side to pick up the subtle differences. Here's a freaky

one: In 2 Samuel 24:1 it says that the Lord incited David to take a census of his troops, which was, in fact, forbidden. So when David complied with the Lord's prompting, he and all Israel were punished. That may seem unfair to you that God would prompt David to sin and then punish him for it. It gets worse: 1 Chronicles 21:1 says, "Satan rose up against Israel and incited David to take a census of Israel." So who prompted David to sin? God or Satan?! Apparently God used Satan to cause David to stumble, and this was in response to Israel's sin which needed to be punished. WOW! You can see now why parallel passages get rather interesting.

Four other books as well have substantial synoptic overlap: Ephesians and Colossians are so close that many scholars believe they were written and delivered at the same time. And the book of Galatians, while not quite a synoptic, appears to be a brief rendition of the book of Romans.

Comparison of Ephesians and Colossians		
Description	Ephesians Text	Colossians Text
Commended for their faith and their love	Eph. 1:15	Col. 1:4,8
Paul prays for their knowledge of the Lord to increase (spiritual wisdom/understanding)	Eph. 1:17	Col. 1:9-10
Paul desires for them to know the will of God	Eph. 5:17	Col. 1:9
Initial emphasis on the redemption found in the sacrifice of Christ	Eph. 1:7	Col. 1:14
Christ is head of his body, the Church	Eph. 1:22-23	Col. 1:18,24
Body metaphor used to explain/exhort the churches' functionality	Eph. 4:15-16	Col. 2:19
Jesus is exalted over all earthly authorities and principalities	Eph. 1:21	Col. 1:16-17
Emphasis on the entrance into God's kingdom from their previous status	Eph. 2:1-10	Col. 1:13,21-22
Description of the plight of the law of Moses	Eph. 2:14-15	Col. 2:14-16
Strong call to holiness	Eph. 4:17–5:13	Col. 3:1-17
Emphasis on the strengthening by the Spirit of God	Eph. 3:16; 4:23-24	Col. 3:9-10
Emphasis on forgiving one another	Eph. 4:32	Col. 3:13
Emphasis on loving one another	Eph. 5:2	Col. 3:14
Strong emphasis on submission	Eph. 5:21–6:9	Col. 3:18–4:1
Tychicus named as carrier of message	Eph. 6:21	Col. 4:7
Paul's prayer request that he might be able to preach the gospel	Eph. 6:19	Col. 4:2

Also, some sections from one book were just flat 'plagiarized' in another book. First Chronicles 1:17-23 is a genealogy borrowed from Genesis 10:21-31 and 11:10-27. And which came first, Psalm 18 or 2 Samuel 22? They are twins! Isaiah 36–39 is nearly a verbatim rendition of 2 Kings 18–20. And Jeremiah 52 is a mirror image of 2 Kings 24–25. All of these fall into the category of 'synoptic' parallels whose 'shades' are substantially the same.

(2) **Old Testament Quotes**. Much of the New Testament is composed of Old Testament material. Approximately 10% of the actual words in the New Testament are directly from the Old Testament, though it is really difficult to make an accurate count. After all, the ancient world did not think like we do about exact reproduction. They didn't have Xerox machines or word processing, but rather they used cumbersome scrolls which were read to audiences who were dominantly illiterate. Because of this different cultural setting, accuracy was measured at the macro level rather than the micro level. They paid attention to the development of stories and broad swaths of theology; we pay attention to exact wording and verse references. The bottom line is that most of the quotes in the New Testament are inexact wording but excellent representations of meaning.

A second problem in quantifying the amount of Old Testament material in the New is that sometimes it looks like the reference is straight from the LXX (Septuagint Greek) and other times it looks like a translation or paraphrase of the MSS text (Massoretic Hebrew). So we are really trying to compare the Greek New Testament with Old Testament in two different languages. That gets slippery as you might imagine.

A third problem is that sometimes they were citing directly from the Old Testament, sometimes they were paraphrasing loosely (as preachers often do), sometimes they were simply making an allusion without attempting any kind of textual parallel, and sometimes these New Testament authors were so steeped in the Old Testament that their own vocabulary began to merge with that of the Bible. This makes it nearly impossible to know just how much of the New Testament is direct quotation, how much is loose reference, and how much is borrowed vocabulary.

Borrowed Biblical Vocabulary

Mary's Magnificat (Luke 1:46-55) contains sixteen phrases
that find strong parallels in dozens of places in the Old Testament.
However, it most closely matches the terminology of Hannah's prayer (1 Sam 2:1-10):

Mary's Magnificat	Hannah's Prayer
My soul magnifies the Lord.	My heart exalts in the Lord.
My spirit rejoices in God my savior.	My strength is exalted in my God.
He has scattered the proud in the thoughts of their hearts.	Let not arrogance come from your mouth.
He has brought down the powerful from their thrones, and lifted up the lowly.	The bows of the mighty are broken, but the feeble gird on strength.
He has filled the hungry with good things, and sent the rich away empty.	Those who were full have hired themselves out for bread, but those who were hungry are fat with spoil.
For he has looked with favor on the lowliness of his servant. Surely, from now on all generations will call me blessed.	The barren has borne seven, but she who has many children is forlorn.

Having said that, however, some things we do know. There are at least 295 Old Testament quotes in the New Testament and 224 of those are prefixed with an introduction such as "it is written" or "in the words of the prophets" or some such thing. Of those quotations, 94 are from the Pentateuch, 99 from the Prophets, and 94 are from the Writings. Thus, there is a fairly even distribution across the Old Testament, indicating that the whole Old Testament played a part in the theological development and writing of the New Testament. The only six Old Testament books not quoted are Ruth, Ezra, Nehemiah, Esther, Ecclesiastes, and Song of Songs. That does not mean these books were not cherished or respected, it just means there was not, apparently a great need to quote them for New Testament doctrine. [Seriously, when was the last time *you* had an opportunity to cite one of these books in a conversation? OK, so Nehemiah has some good leadership sermons, Ecclesiastes is decent for the Christian Goth sub-culture, and Song of Songs works as the butt of jokes (pardon the pun). But realistically,

*The Jewish OT **TaNaK** is divided into three parts:*

Torah *or 'Law' contains the first five books of the OT.*
Nebiim *or 'Prophets' includes Joshua through Kings (excluding Ruth and Daniel).*
Kethubim *or 'writings' have 1 Chronicles through Song of Songs plus Ruth, Lamentations, and Daniel.*

you can understand why they weren't foundational for the early church.]

We also know that every book in the New Testament has some quote from the Old except Philemon and 1–3 John. Matthew, Acts, Romans, and Hebrews have the most quotations and Revelation is packed with an unbelievable number of allusions to the Old Testament, over five hundred by some counts. The bottom line: You have to pay attention to the shadows of the Old Testament in the New because the 'shades' are so close.

Revelation and OT Allusions

It has been correctly suggested that the key to understanding the images of the book of Revelation is by mining the Old Testament allusions that give these images meaning. In 404 verses of the book of Revelation, there are over 500 OT allusions (though some would estimate as many as 850!). For a thorough look at the OT allusions behind each of the verses of Revelation see: Robert Lowery, *Revelation's Rhapsody: Listening to the Lyrics of the Lamb – How to Read the Book of Revelation* (Joplin, MO: College Press, 2006), appendix A.

(3) **Chronological Parallels** may have very different colors on the theological palette. However, the fact that they were written at the same time, allows the reader to put together a matching ensemble that looks very nice. For example, Paul wrote most of his letters during the chronological period described between Acts 15 and 28. If you can read them together, you have, on the one hand, Paul's biography in Acts, and on the other hand, you read his 'diary.' Or put differently, the book of Acts tells you what Paul *did* while his Epistles tell you what Paul *thought*. Here is just one minor example of dozens possible. In Acts 16 we learn that the church of Philippi was started when Paul preached to a group of women down by the river Gangites. This likely indicates that there were not enough Jewish men in the area to establish a synagogue (ten were needed). So these Jewish women were simply worshiping God the best they knew how. What implications does that have for this fledgling church? Two things come to mind. First, Paul refers to the financial generosity of these women on several occasions, but it is particularly touching in Philippians 4:15-18:

> Moreover, as you Philippians know, in the early days of your acquaintance with the gospel, when I set out from Macedonia, not one church shared with me in the matter of giving and receiving, except you only; for even when I was in Thessalonica, you sent me aid again and again when I was in need. Not that I am looking for a gift, but I am look-

ing for what may be credited to your account. I have received full payment and even more; I am amply supplied, now that I have received from Epaphroditus the gifts you sent. They are a fragrant offering, an acceptable sacrifice, pleasing to God.

Yet another implication of this feminine church was some bit of squabbling which Paul addressed directly in 4:2-3: "I plead with Euodia and I plead with Syntyche to agree with each other in the Lord. Yes, and I ask you, loyal yokefellow, help these women who have contended at my side in the cause of the gospel, along with Clement and the rest of my fellow workers, whose names are in the book of life." Volumes could be written on the advantages of reading Acts alongside the Epistles, but these simple illustrations should whet your appetite for more.

The book of Psalms also provides chronological parallels with some of the historical books. In fact, there are places in the Torah where blank spaces are left in the manuscripts and some Rabbis suggest this was for considering Psalms along with that particular historical narrative. Be that as it may, many of the Psalms themselves have specific titles that refer back to incidents, especially in the life of David. Reading the two texts in tandem offers obvious insights into the heart of David.

Psalm	Historical Book	Incident
3	2 Sam 15:13-14	David was fleeing from Absalom
18	2 Sam 22:1-51	David flees from Saul
34	1 Sam 21:13	David acts insane before Abimelech, King of Gath
51	2 Sam 11:4; 12:1	David is caught with Bathsheba
52	1 Sam 21:7; 22:9	Doeg the Edomite informs Saul that David is with Ahimelech
54	1 Sam 23:19; 26:1	Ziphites inform Saul that David was hiding among them
56	none	When the Philistines seized Gath
57	1 Sam 22:1; 24:3	When David fled from Saul into a cave
59	1 Sam 19:11	Saul sent men to watch David's house to kill him.
60	2 Sam 8:13	David fights at Aram Naharaim and Aram Zobah; Joab kills twelve thousand Edomites in the valley of Salt

A third chronological parallel, almost too overwhelming to mention, is the prophetic material which overlaps with the books of 1 and 2 Kings and 1 and 2 Chronicles. Many of the prophetic books tell you exactly when they wrote. Isaiah, for example, opens his book with these words: "The vision concerning Judah and Jerusalem that Isaiah son of Amoz saw during the reigns of Uzziah, Jotham, Ahaz and Hezekiah, kings of Judah." Likewise Jeremiah 1:2-3 says, "The word of the LORD came to him in the thirteenth year of the reign of Josiah son of Amon king of Judah, and through the reign of Jehoiakim son of Josiah king of Judah, down to the fifth month of the eleventh year of Zedekiah son of Josiah king of Judah, when the people of Jerusalem went into exile." Ezekiel (1:1-3) is even more specific:

> In the thirtieth year, in the fourth month on the fifth day, while I was among the exiles by the Kebar River, the heavens were opened and I saw visions of God. On the fifth of the month—it was the fifth year of the exile of King Jehoiachin— the word of the Lord came to Ezekiel the priest, the son of Buzi, by the Kebar River in the land of the Babylonians.

Many of the prophets, in fact, identify their ministry with chronological precision in the first sentence or two of their book: Daniel, Hosea, Amos, Micah, Zephaniah, Haggai, Zechariah. This is obviously not the place to draw out a biblical chronology which others have done with some bit of precision.[1] Yet, when you set out to read either the historical books or the prophetic books you should find out who was living and speaking to each other.

(4) **Prophetic Vocabulary and Symbols**. Every 'guild' has its vocabulary whether athletics, economics, fashion, or fishing. Certain words and symbols mean something that is unique to that profession. For example a hook is different for a fisherman, a boxer, an advertiser, and a basketball player. The prophets likewise have certain ways of talking. For example, what does it mean in Matthew 24:29 when it says the "sun will be darkened"? Is that

---

[1] Check out http://skylardesign.com/clients/oldsites/holman/assets/pdfs/bstudies/chart-of-kings.pdf or http://www.abideinchrist.com/messages/chronisr.html.

really a cataclysmic solar event? Actually, this kind of language is used on a number of occasions in the Old Testament to speak of the downfall of nations (Isa 13:10; 34:4; Joel 2:10,31; Zeph 1:15). The 'sun' or 'moon' refers to a king and his nation, not the solar system. Would it not, therefore, make sense to interpret it in the same way in Revelation 6:12-13; 18:12? Again, if the four beasts of Daniel 7:1-8 represent four different nations which ruled the world consecutively in ancient times, would it not be natural to read the beasts of Revelation 13:2 in the same way? Terms such as 'day of the Lord,' 'last days,' 'abomination of desolation,' etc., appear to be common coin among the prophets. In addition, colors, numbers, animals, and other symbols tend to have similar meanings whether they are found in the Old Testament or in the New.

(5) **Topical parallels**. Perhaps the most important parallels are those that *don't* use the same words but still talk about the same ideas. For example, a collection of all the texts that talk about divorce, war, family, the second coming, or conversion can form the foundation of a well-grounded theology. Difficult subjects like predestination, eternal security, or millennialism can only be dealt with fairly if we hear the whole counsel of God, not just those passages that happen to say what we already believe. Sometimes these topics will have a key word that pops up in two or more texts (cf. "Christian" in Acts 11:26; 26:28; 1 Peter 4:16). More often, however, it is the thoughts rather than the vocabulary that is similar (cf. Matt 10:37 & Luke 14:26; also Luke 16:25 & Rev 6:11).

How to Find Parallels

Now that we know what parallels to look for, how do we find them? There are a number of effective sources for finding parallel passages.

(1) **Read the Bible**. No, really, read your Bible! As you do, make lists of verses you run across that speak to topics you are interested in. For example, if you are interested in women's roles, just find an empty page in the back of your Bible and write the words "Women's Roles." Then, every time you run across a verse about women doing something for the Lord, just jot down the ref-

erence. You will be amazed how quickly your list grows as you go to church, have your devotions, and prepare for lessons. The two drawbacks of this method is that it will take years before your list is close to comprehensive and second, you can only concentrate on three or four lists at a time.

(2) **Use the marginal notes**. A good study Bible will put parallel passages in the margins or in footnotes. These are prepared by professional scholars who know the Bible really well. While they may miss a few texts that you would include or perhaps include a couple you don't think are relevant, they generally are extremely helpful and are a quick way of getting two or three parallel passages for any text. The problem, however, is that they are not designed to deal well with topical parallels nor are they comprehensive due to space limitations.

Here is how you use the Study Bible Features: 1) Notice that the page is cut in two with a solid horizontal line. This division places the biblical text at the top of the page with study notes on the particular text at the bottom of the page. The study notes are helpful insights from biblical scholars on particular aspects of the biblical text that will help you in your study. It is important to remember that while the study notes are very helpful, they are not infallible and should not be looked at as inspired gospel. 2) Notice the top portion of the page is divided in half as well, with a column clearly distinguished in the middle of the biblical text. This column is the parallel passage section of the study Bible that labels important texts that parallel the text you are studying. If you come across a small, italicized letter in superscript (like this: John[e]) then you know that there is a corresponding parallel passage. 3) If there is a small, boldfaced letter in superscript (like this: John[k]), then you will want to reference the bottom right portion of the top half of the page for some textual notes on the passage referenced.

Utilizing these tools and features of the Study Bible can benefit your Bible study immensely . . . so USE THEM!

(3) **Use a topical Bible**. Some Bibles are specifically designed to help you get at parallel passages. The *Thompson Chain Reference Bible* is the best known. Also, some books collect pas-

sages according to topics. **Naves Topical Bible** is the classic standard and fortunately it is free to use online.[2] Other helpful reference works that you could use as well: a scholarly commentary on a Bible book or a theological dictionary that will discuss important topics in alphabetical order. Keep in mind, however, the whole point is to let the Bible comment on the Bible. Don't allow these other books to supplant the reading of God's Word. Allow these other references to function as a walking stick to support you but not as crutches that substitute for your own leg work.

(4) **A Computer Concordance**. We have already talked about the use of a computer concordance as a tool for word studies. It is equally valuable for parallel passages. The real advantage of the computer concordance (aside from speed) is the ability to look up phrases, not just words. In fact, you can look up multiple words in any order by typing in "Jesus AND Christ AND Lord." This will pick up every use of "Lord, Jesus Christ," "Christ Jesus our Lord," "Jesus Christ is Lord," etc. You need to play with this. Let's say you want to investigate miracles. You could type in "Miracle* OR heal*"and you would get every instance of "miracle," "miracles," "heal," "heals," "healing," "healer," etc. This would give you plenty to read. As you read, take note of other synonyms such as "miraculous," "awe," "wonder," "saved," etc. Add these to your search, and in a matter of minutes, you could collect quite a repository of biblical texts on the subject.

Guidelines for Interpretation

Now that you know what you are looking for and know how to find it, how do you interpret parallel passages? Finding parallel passages often requires more art than science. However, interpreting them requires more science than art. Here are some rational guidelines that will help you deal appropriately with parallel passages.

> *Axiom of Parallel Passages:* **Your theology will end at the text with which you begin.**

(1) **Don't abuse lists of Scripture**. How would one abuse a list? First, we arrange lists unfairly. What I mean is that we put our

---

[2] http://bible.crosswalk.com/Concordances/NavesTopicalBible/.

pet passages up front and/or at the very end. The result is that our readers/hearers get the emphasis we want them to receive rather than the emphasis that is actually found in the Bible. For example, if we believe one can fall away, we will present those passages up front and/or end our presentation with a crescendo of 'free-will' texts. This arrangement obscures the 'security texts' so it looks like they are less prominent than they actually are. Conversely, if we believe in eternal security, we present most powerfully those passages that support this position and proceed to explain why the 'freewill' texts don't actually mean what they appear to be saying. It's OK to present your position. It is OK to try to persuade others of your position. It is OK to arrange the Scriptures in a logical order.

But by all means, allow your hearers to hear *all* the Scriptures on a topic, even those that seem to contradict your views. In short, don't use texts as pretexts for your position. Don't proof-text and then pretend that you have taught the whole counsel of God.

> *If you want to challenge your own theological presuppositions, start with theologians who take a different stance than you. Giving others the **first** hearing is often the best way to give others a **fair** hearing.*

So how can I make sure that I present my list of Scriptures fairly? First, prioritize later revelation over earlier revelation. In other words, the prophets will preach Christ more clearly than the patriarchs, and the Epistles will interpret Jesus after his ascension with more clarity than the disciples do in the Gospels while they were still under the Mosaic Law. In short, later revelation is often clearer and fuller than earlier revelation and should, therefore, get priority. In addition, you should prioritize the plain texts, and then move to the obscure. Case in point: Revelation is probably not the place to start your presentation of the end of the world. Rather, start with Jesus' clear teaching on his return or Paul's equally clear statements about end times in the Epistles. By all means, get to Revelation! But allow the plain text to speak first. Let the clear explain the obscure not vice versa. This would include giving priority to prosaic teaching over poetic or parabolic. Literal texts tend to be clearer and more straightforward than nonliteral texts which often emphasize emotions through metaphors.

Second, repeated passages should get priority over single

texts. Now, obviously, if God says something once, that is enough. He really shouldn't have to repeat himself. However, if he does, we should probably pay particularly close attention. This is not dissimilar to your dad telling you to take out the trash. You really should do it the first time, but certainly by the third or fourth time he asks, you're pressing your luck if he catches you sprawled out in front of the TV. Likewise, lots of commands surface once or twice, but when God repeats himself, he is revealing his heart and we had better listen. For instance, the Great Commission is found five times—once in each Gospel and again in the book of Acts. We'd best be about his business. This is not a commission we should get caught procrastinating.

Third, allow each text to stand on its own. Don't force one passage to conform to another. If there is a paradox or even an apparent contradiction, so be it. It is better to allow the context of each passage to determine the A.I.M. than it being determined by an artificial theological system. In other words, really allow texts to speak their piece. Don't push 'round' texts into 'square' theological boxes. I would rather have a schizophrenic theological system than a string of proof-texts abducted from their native contexts. Furthermore, authors write books, not verses. Hence, you must never ignore the meaning of the whole book when you excerpt small passages into a theologically organized list.

Fourth, don't force a text to stand next to another if it doesn't want to. In other words, not all texts are parallel even if they have very similar wording. It is unfair to use a text for your 'topical' collection or theological arrangement just because it happens to say what you want it to. In other words, play fair. Make sure that the context of your text supports the role you are asking it to play in your topical list. Bible study should be honest, not convenient.

Genre Matters for Lists TOO!

Sometimes the genre can play a major role in the interpretation of a list within a text as well. For example, the book of Revelation is written in the genre of apocalyptic literature, which uses a lot of symbolic language. As a result, Revelation 6:15 lists the following people as cowering from God's wrath at the breaking of the sixth seal: 1. kings of the earth, 2. princes, 3. generals, 4. rich, 5. mighty, 6. slaves, and 7. free men. Utilizing the number 7 in naming the groups (which is a symbol for completion in the Jewish mind stemming from the 7 days of creation in which God completed his work), the author is emphasizing the judgment of the complete members of rebellious humanity. But I could add a few names to the list from my own vantage. The list is representative, not comprehensive.

Finally, be cautious about lists. No list in the Bible is comprehensive (not even the genealogies). Lists of sins don't include every transgression. Lists of gifts don't contain every possible work of the Holy Spirit. The two lists of qualifications of elders and deacons are both incomplete: 1 Timothy 3 differs from Titus 1. Does that mean that the two churches had different requirements for leadership? Of course not. These two lists are designed to paint a portrait, not create a checklist. Even if the two lists are combined, they are still not comprehensive. Simply put, combining the lists of qualifications won't give you a sufficient 'check list.' To use another example, many teachers combine the gift lists of Ephesians 4, 1 Corinthians 12, and Romans 12 and ask people to 'find their gift.' However, your gift might not be there. Many people have none of the listed gifts but are incredibly gifted by the Holy Spirit in music, counseling, humor, writing, painting, or any number of other God-honoring, body-building skills. These lists provide us a portrait of the *kinds* of gifts available, the *kinds* of qualifications necessary, the *kinds* of sins to eschew. They are not snapshots frozen in time, but portraits which sketch general outlines.

(2) **Harmonize appropriately Scriptures that appear to stand in contradiction.** Some texts just seem to contradict one another. For example, Mark 15:25 says Jesus was crucified at the 3rd hour (9 a.m.). How can that be when John 19:14 says Jesus was standing before Pilate at the 6th hour (12 noon)? Why does Matthew's genealogy (ch. 1) differ so significantly from Luke's (ch. 3)—these are not the same family tree! Why does Matthew 20:20 say Salome asked for chief seats for her boys but Mark 10:35 gives credit to the sons of Thunder?

Don't kid yourself, there are some real problem passages in the Bible. Don't just explain them away (or worse, simply ignore them). Almost all of the apparent contradictions have reasonable explanations, but frankly, some do not. This may say more about our ignorance of lost historical data than it does about any insufficiency on the part of the text. However, to be fair, we need to admit that some sticky problems just won't be wished away. At the same time, I'm not really in a mood to just roll over and wave a white flag because some half-cocked blogger claims that the Bible is full of errors.

Here are some guidelines for handling discrepancies whether they are from Socrates, Saul of Tarsus, or Shakespeare. These are generally accepted rules-of-fair-play by historians. First, if the author has a track record for honesty and credibility, make every effort to reconcile his/her accounts. In other words, give authors the benefit of the doubt. Second, if a reasonable explanation exists, even if it includes conjecture, the author cannot be charged with an error. This is particularly true since they were a lot closer to the situation than we—that puts them in a better position to evaluate and present the data. Third, he who asserts must also prove. If a skeptic says the Bible is in error, it is up to him/her to show where and how. So if someone claims there are errors in the Bible, ask him to show you not only where the error is, but that there is no reasonable explanation for the supposed discrepancy. Fourth, only if one account confirms what another denies can we be sure of an error. In other words, it takes mutually exclusive accounts to be irreconcilable. In the third example above, Salome (in Matthew) and James and John (in Mark) ask for chief seats. That is not a contradiction but variation in telling the story. All three of them participated in the request. So what if Matthew emphasizes the mother while Mark does not?! To call this a contradiction is not just silly, it is petty and mean. In other words, play nice. An author is innocent until proven guilty. That doesn't mean we gullibly accept everything at face value. But where authors write ostensibly historical narratives, you can assume that they both attempt and are capable of 'getting it right,' at least with the big stuff.

Summary

Parallel passages are a powerful way of allowing the Bible to be your first and best commentary on itself. Since God is the author of the whole collection, it just makes sense to see what he said elsewhere in this continuing conversation. As long as we are aware of what he said first, what he said most often, and what he said most clearly, we can fairly develop a collection of texts on certain topics which provide a holistic view of God's perspective on important doctrines. Furthermore, with a few key tools at our fingertips, and a few principles for organizing our findings, this task of collecting parallel passages is well-within the grasp (and responsibility) of every Bible student.

The Difference between Historical Research, Word Studies, and Parallel Passages

All three of these will look quite a bit alike. They will all use parallel passages and all three will be in paragraph form with a word or phrase highlighted at the upper left of the paragraph. However, each addresses different issues and asks different questions.

Historical Research is an attempt to reconstruct the biblical world. We want to ask the six investigative questions (who, what, where, when, why, how), especially about tangible historical artifacts. We want to draw verbal pictures (sometimes even including literal pictures) of the things we are speaking about. The parallel passages are used in this section to show how the historic artifact actually functioned in the real world. We are using the Bible as a primary source of data. Major resource will be Bible encyclopedias.

Word Studies are an attempt to define a word within its contexts. To do this we will draw upon dictionary definitions, usage, and context. Our first task is to establish a "range of meaning." In other words, how was the word actually used? Dictionaries, etymology, translations, etc. will all be helpful. But primarily parallel passages are used here to demonstrate what this word was used to mean by various authors. Then we zero in on our own passage to show how the word was used in *this instance.* Major resources will include concordances and lexicons (foreign language dictionaries).

Parallel Passages are used to develop a theological synthesis of ideas (such as grace, faith, hell, sovereignty, etc.). We are not necessarily concerned here with specific words or artifacts but with ideas. We want to draw up a logical argument, a theological synthesis on what the counsel of God through the Bible has to say pertaining to our particular subject. Think of it as developing a statement of faith supported by God's word. Major resources will be marginal cross-references, topical Bibles, and theological dictionaries.

Going Further:

Assignments and Further Reading

Assignment #15:

For this assignment, you will need to find all of the parallel passages for your text.

Write a commentary on your text using nothing but parallel passages. This is not a comprehensive commentary, but one which addresses specific theological issues that arise either from words/phrases or from ideas in your text. Each theological subject should be treated separately in its own paragraph like the earlier project of Historical Background. Think in terms of 100 passages quoted, cited, or summarized through statistics.

The idea for this assignment is for you to develop a commentary on your text using nothing but the Bible. The rewards for pouring yourself into this task will pay great dividends because you will be able to allow the Bible to interpret the Bible without the persuasion of commentators who oftentimes carry a bias that can pull you away from what the text may actually be saying. Instead, dive in and allow the Bible to illuminate itself allowing the A.I.M. to blossom in its canonical context.

The Art and Discipline of Application

8

Why do you call me, "Lord, Lord," and do not do what I say? I will show you what he is like who comes to me and hears my words and puts them into practice. He is like a man building a house, who dug down deep and laid the foundation on rock. When a flood came, the torrent struck that house but could not shake it, because it was well built. But the one who hears my words and does not put them into practice is like a man who built a house on the ground without a foundation. The moment the torrent struck that house, it collapsed and its destruction was complete. (Luke 6:46-49 NIV)

To plagiarize 1 Corinthians 13: If I memorize the entire Bible and read Greek and Hebrew but do not apply it to my life, I know nothing. If I understand theology, philosophy, and sociology but do not live out the words in the text, I prove nothing. If I fathom all mysteries and solve all problem passages, but do not love God or my fellow man better, I accomplish nothing!

Hermeneutics, as you will recall, comes from the messenger god Hermes. His task was to *tell* the message, not merely to *understand* it. Likewise, the job of the biblical interpreter is not to be smarter but to faithfully apply the written message of God to the community of his people. This can sometimes be a problem, because the very interest that drives us into deeper study of the Bible can isolate us from contemporary concerns. This happens

135

with a lot of 'special interest' groups. For example, those noble science-fiction buffs who faithfully attend 'Star Trek' conventions (let's be honest now) are sometimes just weird. It is as if they actually believe Klingon is a real language. Their peculiar interest in science fiction can divorce them from the reality of contemporary life. This can be equally true for cricket fans, bridge clubs, or fanatics of certain reality TV shows. They are so 'into it' that they are 'out of touch.' Preachers are often just as out of touch. They use strange terms such as 'predestination,' 'atonement,' and 'sanctification.' They pray in King James English. And they know more about what was going on in Babylon at 586 B.C.E. than they know about Baghdad today. Perhaps we should follow the advice of the German theologian Karl Barth who suggested that proper Bible study could only be done with a Bible in one hand and a newspaper in the other.

Clear back in the fourth century, Augustine got it right when he said that the goal of all Bible study was to love God and love one's neighbor. Application that deviates from those two primary commands is in danger of deviance. It is possible, you know, to be an orthodox heretic by knowing all the correct doctrines but having the wrong attitudes and actions. In short, the end of Bible study is not just the head but always the hands and heart.

> Purpose of Studying
> the Bible
>
> **II**
>
> Transformation in Love
> (Love God and Others More)

Before getting into the actual principles for proper application, there is one warning sign we must observe: **If your application exceeds the AIM of the text, your interpretation ceases to share God's authority.** In other words, if you make a promise that the text does not make, God is not obligated to fulfill that promise; after all, it is your promise not his. Or if you espouse a doctrine that is extrabiblical, your fellow Christians are not obliged to agree or follow your teaching. Or if you give an opinion that the inspired writers do not share, your hearers need not follow your example.

Perhaps an illustration or two would help. Some preachers promise health and wealth if you will just have enough faith in God (and perhaps contribute a few shekels to their coffers). What does this say about the faithful Christians, many of whom are martyrs, living with torture and poverty in places like China, Sudan, or Haiti? Clearly the doctrine exceeds the biblical message and therefore is irrelevant at best and deceptively destructive at worst. Here's another example: A preacher says that you are sinning against God if you dance (or go to movies, date, listen to rock & roll, get a tattoo, etc. *ad nauseum*), but there is no clear biblical text to back it up. Then you fellowship with Christians from another church or meet other Christians on a missions trip who practice such things. Are they hell-bound? If the Bible is used to prohibit certain behaviors that the text really does not speak against, then the judgment of man is at play not the judgment of God. Certainly illustrations such as this could abound, but these will suffice to make the point: If your application exceeds the AIM of the text, it ceases to share God's authority. It may still be a good application in certain contexts and it may even produce good fruit, but it is always tenuous territory when we try to say more than the Bible itself says.

The Target of Application

As the following chart shows, there are three target areas for application: head, heart, and hands. What the chart doesn't show is that a text can be applied in three directions: (1) to you personally, (2) to your local congregation, and/or (3) to the church universal. This does NOT mean that every text should have nine distinct applications (head/heart/hands of you/the local congregation/the church universal). Though a text could probably have at least one application for you, at least one for your congregation, and at least one for the church universal.

Let's say that you are a selfish person who is hoarding your money, but you attend a wealthy and generous church. If you teach on a text dealing with wealth, it might be appropriate to apply it to the *head* of your congregation (think wisely about how you invest these offerings), to your own *hands* (increase what you give), and to the *heart* of the church universal (our gifts speak of our solidarity with you in Christ). There is an infinite variety of applications like this. Don't think you have to apply every text to all three areas (head, heart, hands) in every direction (you, your congregation, the church universal).

Goal of Application		How to Make Application	
Head: Mind & Will	Isa 55:8-9; Rom 12:1-2	Time & Feeding	Heb 5:11-14
Heart: Spirit & Emotions	2 Cor 3:3	Gift of God and Meditation	1 Cor 1:20–2:16; Ps 1:1-2
Hands: Behavior	Luke 6:46; John 14:21; 1 John 5:2-3	Practice and Wisdom	Jas 1:22-25

Head: Application aimed at the head is not just to teach correct doctrine. While knowing the right 'stuff' is important, it is worse than useless if it doesn't lead to a change of one's will. The fact is, biblical knowledge often makes people legalistic, divisive, and sometimes just downright mean! We somehow feel that if we know more than the next guy, it justifies being judgmental and sectarian. Isaiah 55:8-9 offers a helpful corrective to our own intellectual arrogance:

> *The Two Greatest Tools for Bible Study:*
> **1. Memorization**
> **2. Pencil and Paper**
> *These are more powerful spiritual 'crowbars' than Greek and Hebrew, commentaries, sermons, and concordances all combined!*

"For my thoughts are not your thoughts,
neither are your ways my ways,"
declares the LORD.
"As the heavens are higher than the earth,
so are my ways higher than your ways
and my thoughts than your thoughts."

Our goal is not to be educated but to be transformed: "Do not conform any longer to the pattern of this world, but be transformed by the renewing of your mind. Then you will be able to test and approve what God's will is—his good, pleasing and perfect will" (Rom 12:2).

How does such a transformation of thinking take place? How does one learn to think differently? It is a simple though lengthy process: You eat. That's right, eat. Every day, several times, eat! Listen to how Hebrews 5:11-14 describes the process:

> We have much to say about this, but it is hard to explain because you are slow to learn. In fact, though by this time you ought to be teachers, you need someone to teach you the elementary truths of God's word all over again. You need

milk, not solid food! Anyone who lives on milk, being still an infant, is not acquainted with the teaching about righteousness. But solid food is for the mature, who by constant use have trained themselves to distinguish good from evil.

This doesn't happen overnight. It is a process that takes years. Moreover, don't expect steady, even growth. Education isn't like that. Rather, we leap from one plateau to another. You may read your Bible for a month or two and really not make much progress, but then you will have an 'aha!' moment that puts some pieces of the puzzle together. These moments of revelation don't come as often, however, without the long, tedious process of daily and habitually feeding on God's Word. Here are four very practical steps that will speed your growth:

> "It is the very nature of language to form rather than inform. When language is personal, which it is at its best, it reveals; and revelation is always formative—we don't know more, we become more."
> Eugene Peterson

1. Read the Bible.

I know it sounds too simple to even say, but many people read *about* the Bible in commentaries, magazines, and devotionals but never actually read the text. God chose *Koine* Greek as the language of the New Testament. That was the language of the streets. Even people for whom Greek was their second language could piece it together. In other words, God intends for the Bible to be understood by the common person. So read it. Start with Mark or John if you are completely new to this. Other simple books would include James and Proverbs. The books of Acts and Genesis are also very exciting historical books one must read after the Gospels. And Romans is probably the most important book of Christian doctrine. These are good books to start with. [NOTE: Choose a translation that is easiest for you to read and understand. This will be extremely important in making Bible reading a habitual discipline in your spiritual development. Go to a Bible bookstore or ask your minister; read a chapter or two from three or four different versions. Don't be afraid to even try paraphrases like *The Message*.]

2. Memorize important chapters of the Bible.

That's right, I said *chapters*. Start perhaps with the Sermon on the Mount (Matthew 5–7) or Romans 8. Make a photocopy of it and tape it up in your shower. This will give you a few minutes every day to work on it. Say a phrase out loud over and over again until you can say it completely without looking at the text. Then move to the next phrase.

3. Have a Bible with you at all times.
Read on your lunch break or while waiting in a line. The more you feed the more you'll grow.

4. Serve somebody, somewhere, somehow.
If you only feed and never exercise, you will get fat. You will learn more from your reading if you are giving of your time and implementing your spiritual gifts in service for the body of Christ or the world at large. I'm not merely saying that serving is the *end* of Bible study; I'm saying that serving is the *means* of understanding the Bible better. When we put into practice the principles of the Bible, we will see just how it works.

Heart: Scripture between two leather covers is a rather dead and useless thing. Paul urged the text to be inscribed on the human heart: "You show that you are a letter from Christ, the result of our ministry, written not

WARNING:
It will take you three days before you can really remember a verse without review, and it may take up to 21 days of repetition before it is permanently etched into your memory.

with ink but with the Spirit of the living God, not on tablets of stone but on tablets of human hearts" (2 Cor 3:3). So how do we transfer the text from the page to our heart? There is both a human and divine side to this task.

The human side requires a process called *meditation*. The book of Psalms opens with these words, "Blessed is the man who does not walk in the counsel of the wicked or stand in the way of sinners or sit in the seat of mockers. But his delight is in the law of the LORD, and on his law he meditates day and night." This Hebrew word for 'meditate' indicates something like 'mumbling.' OK, by show of hands, how many of you talk to yourself? I do! (I find this is the best way to win an argument.) This is especially helpful when I'm thinking through an issue. I roll it around in my mind, talk out all sides of it, sometimes even debating with myself.

That, in a nutshell, is meditation. One of the quickest ways to get deep into meditation is not sitting cross-legged and repeating a meaningless chant, but memorizing a text, saying it out loud over and over until those words become a part of the private and internal discussion of your soul.

From the divine side, Scripture is written on your heart through the Holy Spirit. Jeremiah 31:33 says, "'This is the covenant I will make with the house of Israel after that time,' declares the LORD. 'I will put my law in their minds and write it on their hearts. I will be their God, and they will be my people.'" Heart transformation goes beyond your study, cleverness, or intellect, but is dependent on the Spirit of God doing a work in your heart. It requires your heart to be open to the work of God. This means humility, obedience, and love.

This is not a bit of magical hocus-pocus. It is not running around saying "the Spirit told me this and that." Rather, it is much like two people who have been in a very long-standing relationship: Best friends from childhood, twins, or an old married couple. They can finish each other's sentences, communicate volumes with a glance, or pick out just the right gift for Christmas. Why? Because they have come to know the other person by aligning their heart with the 'other.' Our goal is to align our hearts with the Spirit of God so we can know what he is thinking before he even tells us. How do we do that? By listening as moments turn into years and loving as years turn into decades.

Correct hearing has a lot to do with intimate loving. Do you have a favorite teacher or politician? Isn't it true that you listen to them more courteously (overlooking stumbles in speech, giving them the benefit of the doubt, or laughing at jokes that weren't that funny)? If we love God, we learn to listen well, and listening well over a long period of time tends to align our hearts with our beloved.

What this previous paragraph describes is essentially what Paul wrote in 1 Corinthians 1:20–2:16. Could you do me a favor? Pick up your Bible right now and read aloud this passage three times. The first time, simply read the words and get familiar with the sound of it coming out of your mouth. During the second reading, listen to God's voice as it comes through your own—

what is he trying to say? With the third reading, pause after every couple of verses and talk back to God. Ask him questions about the text or make requests for him to do in you what Paul is talking about. This will take at least 10-15 minutes.

Hands. Jesus said, "Whoever has my commands and obeys them, he is the one who loves me. He who loves me will be loved by my Father, and I too will love him and show myself to him" (John 14:21). Later John repeats the sentiment in his first letter, "This is how we know that we love the children of God: by loving God and carrying out his commands. This is love for God: to obey his commands" (1 John 5:2-3a).

Simply put, we don't correctly interpret the Bible until we do what it says. That is not simply to say that we can understand some-

> *Correct* orthodoxy *must lead to* vigorous *orthopraxy.*

thing intellectually but not obey it. I'm suggesting that true understanding involves existential involvement so that you *don't* correctly understand something *until* you practice it.

True story: In my first ministry my wife and I had two children under the age of four. One old codger had been a bachelor all his life but apparently had read some books on rearing children which gave him the right to offer expert advice. For those of you who have yet to procreate, let me simply say that you might encounter a situation or two not adequately explained in the textbooks! All I'm trying to say is that 'book smarts' and 'street smarts' must collide before Bible study is of real value.

So how do you do it? Well, do it! James 1:22-25 offers some pretty good advice:

> Do not merely listen to the word, and so deceive yourselves. Do what it says. Anyone who listens to the word but does not do what it says is like a man who looks at his face in a mirror and, after looking at himself, goes away and immediately forgets what he looks like. But the man who looks intently into the perfect law that gives freedom, and continues to do this, not forgetting what he has heard, but doing it—he will be blessed in what he does.

Studying the Bible is more like learning auto mechanics than theoretical calculus. It is a practical study, designed for action, not merely cognition.

Here is a simple test. Below are instructions and pictures for tying a bowtie [from briteties.com]. Find a bow tie and try to follow along.

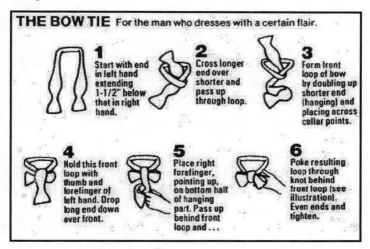

Looks simple doesn't it?! Well, good luck! It is simple . . . once you've actually *done* it. Until then it is mystifying! There is a major difference in reading about something and actually *doing* it. Try this one out: Love your enemies. Or how about this one: Pray without ceasing. Here's an easy one: Do to others as you would have them do to you! (Now that'll take you all day!)

Application Ladder

The following charts will demonstrate how the process of application works. Our goal, simply, is to take a text written to a specific group of people, in a certain place, facing a particular situation and use that text to deal with contemporary issues in our life and time. *Exegesis* pulls principles from the text while *Applica-*

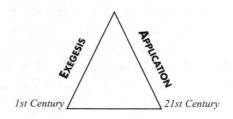

tion places those principles appropriately in modern contexts. Or to put it another way, we draw from a *time bound* text a *timeless truth* for a *timely* situation.

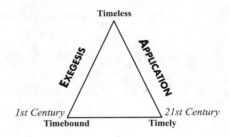

So if we have situations that are similar, we can simply use the text as it stands and apply it to our modern situation. For

example, Christians are still getting married and sometimes have difficulty and separate. Paul spoke to this very situation in 1 Corinthians 7. He said if a believer is abandoned by an unbeliever, the appropriate action is divorce, but if a believer is abandoned by another believer, s/he should pray for reconciliation. Or again in the same letter, Christians were instructed to *not* sue other Christians but to bring the issue to the church for arbitration. That's pretty straightforward stuff.

> *There is only one A.I.M.*
> *There may be several*
> *possible interpretations.*

Well, what if our situations are different? If we move from 1 Corinthians 7 to 11:5, we read, "And every woman who prays or prophesies with her head uncovered dishonors her head — it is just as though her head were shaved." Most women today don't cover their heads like they do in the Middle East. A Muslim woman covering her head today is saying essentially the same thing(s) that Christian women said through this action in the first century. It is a statement of submission, propriety, gender order, etc. If a woman covers her head in church today, is she communicating the same biblical principle? The answer is not an easy one. In some places and times it is 'yes,' and in others it is most certainly 'no.' I'm not trying to solve this problem and say, "Here is what everyone should do." On the contrary, I'm trying to illustrate that this is a problem that does not have easy or fixed solutions.

Where our situation is dissimilar to the biblical world, our best course of action is to discover, as closely as possible, the *principle* being taught in the biblical passage and ask, "How can this principle best be fulfilled in our own place and time?" How do women, for example, most appropriately demonstrate created order, submission, quietness, and propriety?

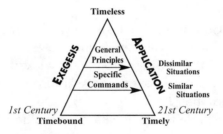

This is the goal of Bible interpretation: to discover these principles and appropriately (and humbly) suggest actions that in our own day will allow the body of Christ to live out the commands and principles inscribed in God's word. The following section will help you draw a distinction between texts that you can apply directly to your life and those that require you to abstract the principle from the text before applying it to contemporary life.

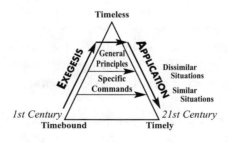

Specific Principles for Applying
Promises, Commands, and Examples

Let's play a little game. In the list below you will find promises, commands, and examples. Place a check mark by those that apply directly to you. We're not talking about principles from the texts that you should contextualize but promises, commands, and examples that directly and straightforwardly apply to you.

Promises:

_____ 1. Exodus 20:5—You shall not bow down to them or worship them; for I, the LORD your God, am a jealous God, punishing the children for the sin of the fathers to the third and fourth generation of those who hate me.

_____ 2. 2 Chronicles 7:14—If my people, who are called by my name, will humble themselves and pray and seek my face and turn from their wicked ways, then will I hear from heaven and will forgive their sin and will heal their land.

_____ 3. Psalm 1:3—He is like a tree planted by streams of water, which yields its fruit in season and whose leaf does not wither. Whatever he does prospers.

_____ 4. Proverbs 22:6—Train a child in the way he should go, and when he is old he will not turn from it.

_____ 5. Jeremiah 33:3—Call to me and I will answer you and tell you great and unsearchable things you do not know.

_____ 6. Mark 16:17-18—And these signs will accompany those who believe: In my name they will drive out demons; they will speak in new tongues; they will pick up snakes with their hands; and when they drink deadly poison, it will not hurt them at all; they will place their hands on sick people, and they will get well.

_____ 7. John 10:28—I give them eternal life, and they shall never perish; no one can snatch them out of my hand.

_____ 8. John 14:26—But the Counselor, the Holy Spirit, whom the Father will send in my name, will teach you all things and will remind you of everything I have said to you.

_____ 9. John 16:24—Until now you have not asked for anything in my name. Ask and you will receive, and your joy will be complete.

_____ 10. Philippians 4:13—I can do everything through him who gives me strength.

What principles helped you make your decision? Do you just claim promises that you like? Or do you only claim the ones you have enough faith to believe? Do you claim those that make sense in your own culture? Well, here are some more hermeneutically *sound* principles that will serve as a guide for which promises you can claim and which ones you probably cannot.

1. Is this in the Old Testament or in the New Testament? Remember, the 'testament' was a 'covenant' or in modern terms a 'contract.' If I say, "I will buy a steak dinner for everyone in my class," I don't expect to have each student bring their significant other, roommate, or grandmother. The deal was with those to whom I made the promise. Exodus 20:5, for example, was a promise that derived straight from the Ten Commandments to Israel and was specifically repealed in Jeremiah 31:29-30 for those under the new covenant. Or again, 2 Chronicles 7:14 was a promise to national Israel. While there may be some principle that would apply to modern Italy or Ecuador, it is doubtful that this is a promise that can be claimed by any and every nation today.

2. In what context was this promise made? John 10:28 is an incredibly wonderful promise for all Christians to claim. However, the context shades the way we should understand it. Originally it was not a promise addressed to Christians; it was a threat to Jesus' opposition which was attempting to steal his disciples. In other words, Jesus is not saying to disciples: "Oh, dear ones, I will look after you." He is staring hard at his enemies who threaten to steal his sheep and says, "Over my dead body!" (Well, even that didn't work). Simply put, we must notice the situation under which this promise was made.

3. To whom was the promise made? Sometimes God made a promise to an individual that should not be applied universally. Jeremiah 33:3 is a case in point. God was not talking to the Christian, nor even to all Israel, but to his specially appointed prophet. Sorry, this is not one that you can claim . . . unless, of course, God has made a similar promise to you personally. But let's be honest, he was talking to Jeremiah.

4. Is the promise conditional or unconditional? When she was about six, my daughter used to call me from work and say, "Daddy, when you get home would you jump on the trampoline with me?" It was great fun for me—for about 10 minutes—but she wanted to go for hours! I couldn't keep up. So I would say, "If your room is clean when I get home, I will jump on the trampoline with you." As you can imagine, that kept me off the trampoline not infrequently. Many (one could almost say 'most') of God's promises are conditional. That is, he says, "If you do what I've asked, then I will give you what I've promised." This was certainly true for God's promise to give the Hebrews the land of Israel. It was theirs to keep . . . as long as they were faithful to his covenant. The Assyrian and Babylonian captivities sufficiently demonstrated that this was not an unconditional promise.

5. Is this promise qualified by other Scripture? John 16:24 looks like an absolute promise: we can ask God for anything and he will give it to us, right? Well, yes, **if** we ask in his name (John 14:13-16), **if** we ask in faith (Matt 21:22), **if** we ask according to his will (1 John 5:14-15), **if** we ask with the right motives (James 4:2-3), and **if** we obey his commands (1 John 3:22). Other passages specifically delimit the conditions of this seemingly unconditional promise.

6. Proverbs are not promises but general principles. They are the way life usually works, but not a guarantee that this is the way life will always work. Some children, for example, who have been brought up in the Lord stray and never come back. That is the unfortunate reality, but it is happily the exception to the rule of Proverbs 22:6.

7. Don't make a promise out of a simple statement of fact. In Philippians 4:13 Paul claims that he can do all things through

Christ. He is not saying that *you* can. With great apologies to all those bumper stickers out there, this is simply not a promise. Furthermore, if we look at the context, Paul is talking about living in any financial state, whether rich or poor, with the help of Jesus. This is hardly about leaping tall buildings, getting back your girlfriend, or passing an exam without actually having studied.

Commands:

Let's play again. Check each of the commands you feel obliged to obey.

_____ 1. Genesis 1:28—Be fruitful and increase in number; fill the earth and subdue it.

_____ 2. Exodus 20:8—Remember the Sabbath day by keeping it holy.

_____ 3. Isaiah 20:2—"Take off the sackcloth from your body and the sandals from your feet." And he did so, going around stripped and barefoot.

_____ 4. Matthew 10:10—Take no bag for the journey, or extra tunic, or sandals or a staff; for the worker is worth his keep.

_____ 5. Matthew 5:22—But I tell you that anyone who is angry with his brother will be subject to judgment. Again, anyone who says to his brother, 'Raca,' is answerable to the Sanhedrin. But anyone who says, 'You fool!' will be in danger of the fire of hell.

_____ 6. Matthew 28:19—Therefore go and make disciples of all nations, baptizing them in the name of the Father and of the Son and of the Holy Spirit.

_____ 7. Acts 15:29—You are to abstain from food sacrificed to idols, from blood, from the meat of strangled animals and from sexual immorality. You will do well to avoid these things.

_____ 8. 1 Corinthians 14:1—Follow the way of love and eagerly desire spiritual gifts, especially the gift of prophecy.

_____ 9. 1 Timothy 2:8—I want men everywhere to lift up holy hands in prayer, without anger or disputing.

_____ 10. James 5:14—Is any one of you sick? He should call the elders of the church to pray over him and anoint him with oil in the name of the Lord.

Again, what principles informed your decision? Do you keep those commands that are culturally comfortable? Those that you are already keeping? Those that sound fun or reasonable? Well, here again are some sound hermeneutical principles for appropriately applying commands.

1. Is this OT or NT? Again, make sure it is part of *your* contract. While the law given to the Israelites has many sound dietary restrictions which would be healthy to follow, as a Christian you are no longer bound to them (Mark 7:19). Be very careful with this principle, however, for while much of the OT law may not be necessary for your salvation, the principles are there for your health, both spiritual and physical. The Sabbath law, for example, which precedes the Jewish code going all the way back to Eden, is not a principle you can afford to ignore. You will rest! You may do it in even increments as God ordained or he will take it all off in one lump sum at the end of your life.

2. Is this a principle to be applied or a law to be obeyed? Paul says that he wants all men everywhere to lift up holy hands in prayer (1 Tim 2:8). Is that a command? Lifting up hands was a common posture of prayer. So it seems that what is being commanded here is prayer. The specific posture does not seem to be the important element. You could be on your knees, with head bowed, or prostrate. The point is to pray, not to lift hands (or so it would seem).

3. Is the law repeated or revoked in the NT? Jesus specifically ordered that his disciples "take no bag for the journey, or extra tunic, or sandals or a staff; for the worker is worth his keep." That was when he sent the twelve out on their first itinerant preaching tour. Later, however, when conditions had changed, he told them to take certain provisions: "But now if you have a purse, take it, and also a bag . . ." (Luke 22:36). Obviously some commands are for certain situations or periods of time. For example, "Be fruitful and multiply" (Gen 1:28); this may be the only command God ever gave that we have actually fully obeyed.

4. Is the law ceremonial or moral? This question is asking about OT laws. Some of them regulated what happened in the temple—sacrifices, washings, festivals, and rituals. Others dealt with ethical issues like marriage, murder, sexual conduct, and property rights. The idea is that we are obligated to live morally under the guidelines of the OT but not necessarily to live according to Jewish traditions or under temple regulations. The general principle is helpful to think about, but in practice gets a bit messy. For instance, is the Sabbath law moral or ritual? Yes, it is something the Jews in particular practiced, but it is a human principle, not just a Jewish practice. Or take circumcision and Kosher rules for food; nothing is more 'Jewish' than these, but they have some health benefits that are undeniable. Consequently, I would suggest that this rule be used not to *eliminate* as much as possible but to *include* as much as possible from the OT. This is more than just 'better safe than sorry'; it is a recognition that the law was God's gift to his people for their benefit, and if we follow it, we will be healthier and happier people, more just to the poor, and more righteous in a wicked world.

> "Moses certainly viewed the revelation of the laws at Sinai as a climactic moment of grace, as did the poet who penned Psalm 119 centuries later. And this is how we should view the law of God, whether it is the law revealed in the Old Testament or the law as it is revealed in the New Testament."
>
> —Daniel I. Block

5. What do common sense, culture, and faith say? Anointing with oil for example (Jas 5:14) was a common medical practice. So when the elders are called to anoint someone, perhaps that was the best medical practice available to them; perhaps today they need to offer scientifically based medical help. (That would be what 'culture' would say.) On the other hand, this passage is surrounded by prayer. So whether the elders offer medical treatment or not, prayer, laying on of hands, and anointing with oil should be practiced. (That's what 'faith' would say.) This is not an argument for what every church should practice but simply an illustration of how this principle can be applied to a very specific command.

Examples:

People did stuff in the Bible. Sometimes the people were bad and we obviously should avoid their example. Sometimes the people were good. Should we follow their example? Mark those examples below that you would feel obligated to follow.

_____ 1. Genesis 14:20—Then Abram gave him a tenth of everything.

_____ 2. 2 Samuel 6:14—David, wearing a linen ephod, danced before the LORD with all his might.

_____ 3. Matthew 26:30—When they had sung a hymn, they went out to the Mount of Olives.

_____ 4. Mark 1:35—Very early in the morning, while it was still dark, Jesus got up, left the house and went off to a solitary place, where he prayed.

_____ 5. John 6:11—Jesus then took the loaves, gave thanks, and distributed to those who were seated as much as they wanted. He did the same with the fish.

_____ 6. Acts 1:26—Then they cast lots, and the lot fell to Matthias; so he was added to the eleven apostles.

_____ 7. Acts 4:32—All the believers were one in heart and mind. No one claimed that any of his possessions was his own, but they shared everything they had.

_____ 8. Acts 13:3—So after they had fasted and prayed, they placed their hands on them and sent them off.

_____ 9. Acts 20:7—On the first day of the week we came together to break bread. Paul spoke to the people and, because he intended to leave the next day, kept on talking until midnight.

_____ 10. 1 Corinthians 16:1-2—Now about the collection for God's people: Do what I told the Galatian churches to do. On the first day of every week, each one of you should set aside a sum of money in keeping with his income, saving it up, so that when I come no collections will have to be made.

Following examples is difficult because we don't often know whether an apostle or saint was doing something with the intention of setting an example or whether they were just going about their daily business with no intention of anyone imitating them. What makes it even more difficult is that most of the examples we have were written by someone other than the person setting the example. So you have to decide not only the intentions of the actor but of the author. There is a second significant difficulty here—culture. Some of the examples we simply cannot follow since yokes, crosses, and camels simply aren't available to most Americans and foot washing, headdresses, and phylacteries have long gone out of style. So here are some principles that will help you discern this very complicated situation.

1. Is the action specifically approved or disapproved? In Acts 4:32 the early Christians shared all their possession with the poor among them. Luke sandwiches this statement between a description of the unity of the church and the power of the Apostles to perform miracles. That, my friend, is a ringing endorsement of this practice.

2. How does the narrative treat the example? Does the author give us any clue as to whether it was a good thing or a bad thing? Is there any contextual clue, characterization, consequences, or explicit statements that paint the action in a good light or in ominous tones? For example, in Acts 1:26 the original Christian church did not know who should replace Judas Iscariot, so they cast lots. That is an Old Testament practice that basically left the decision up to God (or blind luck?). In this instance the lot fell to Matthias and he became an Apostle. While that may sound pretty suspect to us, the fact is, in the next two verses, Matthias was among the Apostles when they received the power of the Holy Spirit. Thus the text itself gives a subtle clue that the decision, on that occasion, was valid.

3. Does this example match any biblical commands? Abraham giving a tenth (Gen 14:20) seems to foreshadow the OT rules for giving a tenth to the Lord. On the other hand, David showing off his BVDs in worship, though approved in the context, is nowhere else commanded (2 Sam 6:14). Likewise, when Jesus prayed for lunch and then distributed the loaves and fishes to 5,000 (John 6:11), that was a good thing, but it is not likely that it is a model for us to follow.

4. How does this align with culture? Remember, our Christian culture must be formed by the Bible, not vice versa. Nevertheless, we do need to ask whether some examples can really be imitated. We probably will not be invited to preach in a synagogue as we enter a new town on a mission trip, but that is what Paul almost always did. Nor can most of us heal lepers miraculously as part of our itinerant preaching ministry. And since the Apostles have all died out, having a counsel where they arbitrate doctrinal issues is out of the question.

5. What does common sense and faith say? Since we now have elders and the indwelling of the Holy Spirit, there are better options for selecting leaders than casting lots. Or night-people will probably do better to pray in the evening rather than getting up early in the morning as Jesus did in Mark 1:35.

6. Are there any patterns? This is perhaps the most important question to ask when determining whether to follow a biblical example. If there is a single instance such as singing a hymn after the Passover meal (Matt 26:30) or taking the Lord's Supper on the first day of the week (Acts 20:7), it is far more difficult to set rules for imitation. Where there are discernible patterns, however, we are on much more secure ground for establishing precedents for behavior. In the book of Acts, for example, we have a number of models of conversion, race relations, leadership development, economic sharing, and submission to the Holy Spirit. So look for patterns not just single examples.

Conclusion

Often we spend the bulk of our time in the first-century world looking at the meaning of words, cultural background, historical setting, etc. Proper application, however, is the primary goal of Bible study, so this step cannot be short-circuited. It does not require the kind of robust intellectual study of the previous steps. Rather, it demands meditation, spiritual sensitivity, and a view of the world around us. Here we have to keep the newspaper as firmly in one hand as we have the Bible in the other. The Scriptures are immensely relevant. They address every major life issue we face in the 21st century, but it will require the wisdom of godly men and women to extract and translate its principles so the modern person can see the personal, powerful, and relevant counsel of God in their lives. You are that person for a waiting and wondering world—waiting for the God of the universe to speak and wondering if his words can make sense of a shattered and broken world. The message of the Bible can speak; we must give it voice.

Going Further:

Assignments and Further Reading

Assignment #16:

✍ Meditate on your text. Put an X in the boxes where you think your text speaks today.

	Head	Heart	Hands
You personally			
Local congregation			
Church Universal			

✍ Now, write out the application for each of these Xs.

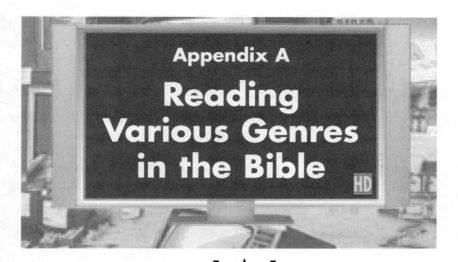

Appendix A

Reading Various Genres in the Bible

HD

When you walk into a video store and look around at the various sections, you see all *kinds* of movies. Down one aisle are comedies, another has romance, the next is horror, then documentary, hot releases, etc. These sections demark the *genre* of the movies. What you're 'into' or in the mood for will determine which section you gravitate to. If you decide on a romantic movie, there is a certain way of watching it, you know. One really should have a 'significant other' on one arm and a box of Kleenex on the other.

> *Genre is a French word meaning 'kind' or 'category.' It refers to the various kinds of literature, music, and art, including books or movies.*

The lights should be low and the mood serene. If you are watching *Monte Python and the Holy Grail*, or *Princess Bride* you want a very different atmosphere. War movies and action flicks (anything with a lot of bombs and gratuitous violence) really need a group of guys and surround sound to make it work. The point is, we know that there is a certain way to watch various kinds of movies.

Likewise, there are right ways and wrong ways of reading various genres of Scripture. The best book on this subject is *How to Read the Bible for All It's Worth*, by Gordon Fee and Douglas Stuart. If you are going to buy one (other) book on hermeneutics, this would be our suggestion. However, we wanted to give you a synthesis of the biblical genres here so you would have the essential rules at your fingertips. In the following charts, we will walk you through the nine major genres of the Bible, giving you their primary characteristics on the left and the interpretive rules called for by these characteristics on the right. Feel free to cut these out of this book and paste them into your Bible for easy reference (no, we don't think they are 'inspired' rules, but they will help you read the inspired word with greater clarity). One final note, the embarrassingly truncated rules you are about to read can be augmented by the online lectures which will hopefully make more sense out of these all-too-brief charts.[1]

---

[1] These lectures can be found at http://markmoore.org/resources/lectures.html, then click on one of the five parts titled "Genre."

#1 Historical Narrative: 1–2 Samuel, 1–2 Kings, 1–2 Chronicles, Judges, Joshua, Acts
These texts make up 40% of the Bible, thus narrative is the most common biblical genre.

Characteristics	Interpretive Rules
1. Biblical history is really HIS-story. It tells how God acts in history. 2. Components to look for in Narrative: 　a. Plot and action—speed, direction, scenes 　b. Characterization—what hats do the players wear? Who are the 'good' and 'bad' guys? 　c. Setting—geography, time, culture, etc. 　d Dialogue or speeches (all narrative gravitates to dialogue, so they are critical) 　e. Narration—who tells the story and how? 3. Contains other Genre—proverbs, riddles, fables, parables, songs, lists, genealogies. 4. There are different types of stories 　a. Tragedy—Samson, Saul, Solomon 　b. Comedy—a happy ending through a dramatic turn of events, such as disguises, providential coincidences, escapes, or surprising turn of events. Examples include Esther and Joseph. 　c. Romance—Ruth 　d. Heroic—Exploits of an individual hero or protagonist (Moses, Abraham, Gideon, David). The hero represents the virtues and vices of the larger community. The book of Judges is a collection of these. 　e. Satire or irony—"Exposure of human vice or folly through ridicule or rebuke" (Jonah; John 21) 　f. Polemic—Elijah's "contest" with 450 prophets of Baal (1 Kgs 18:16-46); 10 plagues. 　g. Reports (3rd person) or Memoir (1st person)—tribal settlements (Jdg 1:16-17); royal building (1 Kgs 7:2-8; 12:25); military campaigns (1 Kgs 14:25-26). The report lets the reader in on the necessary information for understanding the rest of the story. Like an orchestra, the series of events and reports must be read together to hear them correctly.	1. Meaning is in the whole story, its movement, actions, and characters; but it is not explicitly taught. Furthermore, your story is likely only one scene in a larger "play." See how each scene fits together and builds into the whole story. Pay particular attention to how the plot develops and twists (comedy), particularly to the turning points and climax. 2. Characterization is critical. Pay particular attention to each person's relationship with God as well as God's role in the narrative. 3. Endings to stories are particularly important. 4. Speeches provide crucial information to the reader. Pay particular attention to the occasion of the speech and identify its main thrust in a single sentence. 5. How does this individual's life model what our relationship with God should or should not be? 6. Look for values: The hero's and God's. What is the heartbeat of the passage? Caution: God is claustrophobic—don't try to squeeze him into a box. 7. Application should often look for analogous situations between Israel and the Church. Pay particular attention to NT citations or even allusions to your story. If it's not mentioned directly, look for how similar themes are handled (reconciliation, creation, law, sin, etc.)

#2 **Legal:** Exodus 20–40, Leviticus, Numbers 5–6; 15; 18–19; 28–30; 34–35; Deuteronomy	
Characteristics	Interpretive Rules

1. They are deeply tied to the Mosaic covenant. The law has been abrogated (Rom 10:4; Col 2:14; Eph 2:15) as a legal foundation for the church, yet embodied and fulfilled in the person of Christ.
  a. The law is still very much applicable (2 Tim 3:16-17) but must be interpreted through the grid of Jesus' person and work.
  b. The functions of the law are still very much in effect.
    i. Induce guilt by activating one's conscience (Rom 3:19-20)
    ii. To punish those who do evil (although Gentiles are judged by their conscience, not the Mosaic code, and Christians have had their penalty paid).
    iii. It leads us to Jesus (Gal 3:23-25).
    iv. For Christians, however, its primary function is to teach us about the kind of holiness God demands and the depth of relationship he desires to have with us.
    v. There are certain social and physical benefits in following God's laws.
2. Types of legal declarations.
  a. Apodictic—This is a directive or law which is not conditioned: "You shall not" (no exceptions!). Typically these come in a series that is almost poetic, e.g., Ten Commandments.
  b. Casuistic = case by case (e.g., Lev 20:9-18,20-21; Deut 15:7-17). These laws have conditions: "If . . . then." Typically these are grouped by topics, so be sure to investigate the context of the surrounding laws to see how they are categorized.
3. Biblical laws are not comprehensive. They merely give examples of how certain cases were handled that are to be applied to similar cases by godly judges.
	1. To whom is this law given?
	  a. What covenant is it under and what obligations do we have to that covenant?
	  b. Are there cultural considerations or scientific advances that would alter how this law is applied?
	2. What kind of relationship is enforced between God and man through this law?
	  a. These legal codes are not comprehensive, but exemplary. What is the heartbeat of this legislation?
	  b. What kind of holiness does God demand and what kind of relationship does he invite us to?
	3. What does this law teach us about the nature of God and the nature of man?
	  a. These laws are not temporary; their principles endure! What is the timeless truth behind the cultural husk? cf. Lev 19:27-28.
	  b. From Matthew 5:17, all of the OT applies to Christians, but none of it applies apart from its fulfillment in Christ (2 Tim 3:16).
	    i. In some cases the NT is stricter than the OT, e.g., divorce and remarriage.
	    ii. Reiterated laws directly apply to Christians, e.g., love your neighbor, 2-3 witnesses.
	    iii. Some laws still are to be obeyed in principle, though not literally, e.g., Sabbath, cleanliness. Some laws were abolished, e.g., sacrifices (Heb 10:1-10); food laws (Mark 7:19), circumcision (Gal 5:2-6).
	3. In what ways would this contribute to the physical, social, and emotional health of the community of God's people?

#3 **Wisdom Literature:** Job, Proverbs, Ecclesiastes, Song of Songs	
Characteristics	Interpretive Rules
1. Reflective (esp. Job/Eccl)—not necessarily directive: giving things to think about more than rules to follow. They deal with the real issues of life: pain in Job, relationships in Proverbs, the meaning of life in Ecclesiastes, love in Song of Songs. 2. Seasons of Life—the young need Song of Songs, middle-aged need Proverbs, the old need Ecclesiastes. 3. Probable truth—it tells how life generally works. Hence, it is proverbial (Prov 1:33; 3:9-10 [cf. 15:16-17]; 17:2) but should not be taken as promises. 4. Poetic—pay attention to parallelism. 5. The contexts are often unreliable contexts. While Job sustains long arguments, other wisdom books, especially Proverbs are short sayings that may or may not be topically arranged. 6. These are noncovenantal. They apply to all people of all times.	1. Wisdom literature does not always answer "What should we do?" but "What's really going on here?" (e.g., "A fool and his money are soon parted."). So use these books as interpretive lenses for life. 2. General (but not absolute) maxim. Don't make promises out of these sayings. 3. Conclusions are more important than the arguments that lead up to them (Eccl). Pay most careful attention to how these books end.

#4 Gospels: Matthew, Mark, Luke, John	
Characteristics	Interpretive Rules

1. Gospels are a unique genre: a strange mix of history and biography. A great portion of the text is devoted to the death of Jesus which the earlier portions of the text seem to foreshadow.
2. Focus:
  a. Kingdom of God inaugurated by Jesus
  b. Death/Burial/Resurrection of Jesus.
3. Three difficulties:
  a. Jesus did not write any of it.
    i. They were written years after Jesus lived, and much of the material is not only paraphrased but edited to reflect each author's theological interests.
    ii. These literary units were passed on (orally) often without their contexts. Sometimes the contexts were lost (e.g., Acts 20:35) and often these sayings were arranged topically (e.g., Matt 10).
  b. Matthew, Mark, and Luke (Synoptics) look a lot alike, but John is quite different. Thus, we must look not only at the storyline of each individual Gospel but at the parallels in the others which overlap. This provides a great opportunity for additional information but also the great frustration of varying accounts.
  c. Pay attention to both Jesus' audience and the Gospel writers' (e.g., John 6 and the Eucharist). Jesus speaks only through the evangelists' writings, hence he speaks not only to his historical audience but to the churches who read (and read) these accounts.
4. Structure:
  a. Selection—Chosen vignettes from oral preaching (*kerygmatic*) were arranged into a story under the evangelist's management.
  b. Arrangement—chronological, topical, and theological.
  c. Emphasis—each author arranges material to make points important to him.
5. Imbedded Genre: Parables, miracle stories, pronouncement stories, sermons, etc., all of which demand particular interpretive rules.
	1. Three key questions to ask:
	  a. Who is Jesus? What can we learn about him through this story?
	  b. What do Jesus' words and example tell us about loving God and loving our neighbor?
	  c. What is the evangelist trying to teach through structure of his stories? What does his arrangement and redaction add to the story itself?
	2. What is the need of the Christian community that first received these documents as well as those which read them today?
	3. How can I communicate this orally to make Jesus famous as well as exhort the body of Christ to look more like her Lord?
	4. We must read the Synoptics in the shadow of the cross—everything points to the cross and the resurrection. John, however, is to be read in the shadow of the church. What theology and ecclesiology develops from his text?

#5 Acts	
Characteristics	Interpretive Rules

1. Acts is theological history, so everything true about narratives and Gospels also apply to this book, but it has additional features as well.
  a. It has more dates, places, and people who can be confirmed outside the Bible through documents and archaeology than any other book of the Bible.
  b. Miraculous events are imbedded within this historical book demonstrating a worldview in which God interacts in our world.
  c. Selected materials and selective presentation. Luke is the only Gentile writer of the NT and shows a great interest in 'lost' people: Gentiles, women, the sick.
  d. The Holy Spirit is the real hero of the book and in many ways takes over where Jesus left off in the Gospels.
2. Part 2: This is a two-part work along with the Gospel of Luke.
  a. Peter and Paul are featured as the leaders to embody the ministry of Jesus.
  b. This is not just what was but what ought to be. This book tells about the early church which is, in many ways, a model for us to follow in the church today.
  c. We should remember that it is essentially an identical genre to Luke. Look for stories that rely on what has gone before and even shadow previous events.
	1. Historical Precedent . . . to a point
	  a. Stick to the main themes and most often repeated ones.
	  b. Look for characterization and how individuals are represented.
	  c. Follow Luke's larger storyline to discern the main point of the episode, not merely details that say what you want them to.
	  d. Compare this to other NT teachings on the same subject.
	2. Understand the major themes as a paradigm for the modern church:
	  a. The Holy Spirit and power
	  b. Church growth—geographic, ethnic, gender, and leaders through:
	    i. Preaching centered on the resurrection
	    ii. Prayer
	    iii. Suffering
	  c. Comparison of Peter to Paul and Paul to Jesus as the ongoing incarnation.
	  d. Legal innocence, yet social poignancy of Christianity.
	3. Speeches inform the reader how to understand the narrative. Though speeches make up one third of the book, what we have are mere summaries.
	4. Compare it to information in the Epistles. This is a *huge* advantage: Read Acts (Paul's biography) alongside the Epistles (Paul's journal). They inform each other.

#6 Epistles: Romans, 1 & 2 Corinthians, Galatians, Ephesians, Philippians, Colossians, 1 & 2 Thessalonians, 1 & 2 Timothy, Titus, Philemon, James, 1 & 2 Peter, 1, 2, 3 John, Jude

Characteristics	Interpretive Rules

1. These are simply letters written in proper Greco-Roman style: sender, recipient, greeting, thanks/theme, prayer, body, exhortation, closing (prayer/salutation). Although the average Greco-Roman letter was 295 words, the average NT letter was 2,495 words. Together they make up 35% of the NT.
 	
 2. Epistles were written because of specific situations in the church(es) to which they were directed. They were never intended to be exhaustive or systematic doctrinal statements. Hence, care should be taken when drawing principles of behavior from them.
 	
 3. Epistles differ from private letters—these were to be read publicly in church. In addition, they carried with them the authority of the author in the absence of that person.
 	
 4. They were often coauthored by an amanuensis (secretary), who had some freedom to impose his personal style on the letter. This may account for some of the varying styles of Paul's letters or the Greek style of 1 & 2 Peter. They were then hand-delivered.
 	
 5. Some epistles lack formal elements: 1 John, James, 2 Peter. Hebrews looks more like a sermon-brief than a letter.
 	
 6. Epistles have a number of significant subgenres that demand special interpretive principles:
 a. Parenetic—exhortation
 b. Diatribe—hypothetical objections from opponents were considered and answered.
 c. Creeds or hymns (Phil 2:6-11; Col 1:15-20; 1 Tim 3:16)
 d. Lists—first and last items are most important.
	1. Determine the situation that prompted the letter. This is like listening to one end of a telephone conversation—it's difficult to figure out what is going on at the other end. So here are three tricks that will help you 'hear' what is going on behind the scene:
	 a. Read book in one sitting taking notes on
	    i. recipients
	    ii. Paul's attitudes
	    iii. mention of the occasion of writing,
	    and then
	    iv. outline the book.
	 b. Compare to Acts
	 c. Consult commentaries, etc.
	
	 2. Think paragraphs! Don't look merely at individual verses, even if they do make good bumper stickers! Listen to the argument which the author develops in each paragraph and how those arguments 'stack up' one paragraph upon the next. CAUTION: When reading Paul, you need to know he is not opposed to chasing a tangent.
	
	 3. Look for commands to be obeyed and principles to be applied. This may best be done in a group setting. Epistles, more than any other genre, can be applied directly to our situations since they were directed to Christian communities like ours which are trying to live as the body of Christ.

#7 **Poetry:** Psalms	
Characteristics	Interpretive Rules

1. Poetry is found throughout the Bible, especially in prophecy (cf. Exod 15; Judg 5; 1 Sam 2; Luke 1:46-55,67-79; Revelation).
  a. Second most common genre, behind narrative, comprising ⅓ of the OT.
  b. Only seven books in OT have no poetry (Leviticus, Ruth, Ezra, Nehemiah, Esther, Haggai, Malachi; five of these are postexilic).
2. Categories of Poetry: song, liturgy, prayer (some imprecatory); theatrical plays (Job and possibly Song of Songs), prophetic (especially Messianic).
3. Literary devices
  a. Parallelism is the primary literary device of Hebrew poetry:
    i. Synonymous: the first line is repeated in different words by the following line.
    ii. Antithetic: the second line says the opposite of the first.
    iii. Synthetic: the second (and sometime 3rd, 4th, etc.) line builds on what was said in the first.
  b. Figures of speech are dominant in poetry where mountains clap and stars sing, etc.
  c. Compact language—poetry says things in abbreviated lines and often drops 'unnecessary' words such as particles.
4. 116 of the 150 Psalms have titles. Some give historical information, others musical instruction such as the genre of the song or the kind of music which is to accompany the psalm.
	1. Analyze the **structure** and literary craft of the poem. Use the parallelism as a crowbar for interpretive leverage to understand the author's ideas.
	2. Understand the **emotions** behind the words. Remember, poets don't write essays, they paint pictures. Tap into the artistic side of your brain. Psalms that deal with life experiences or with one's relationship with God are nondispensational.
	3. If possible, determine the **historical** situation out of which the Psalm arose.
	4. Handle **figures** of speech carefully, especially hyperbole and metaphor.
	5. Read and sing these aloud. Also use these poems liturgically and even musically. It is not merely the message that is inspired but also its **method** of delivery which was musical and corporate.
	6. OT poetry is filled with **Christology**—look for Jesus.

#8 Prophecy: 5 major (Isaiah, Jeremiah, Lamentations, Ezekiel, Daniel) and 12 minor prophets describe the size of the books, not their importance.

Characteristics	Interpretive Rules

1. Prophecy is more pastoral than predictive. Fee & Stuart say, "Less than 2 percent of the Old Testament prophecy is messianic. Less than 5 percent specifically describes the New Covenant age. Less than 1 percent concerns events yet to come" (*How to Read the Bible for All It's Worth*, p. 166). Most prophecy is for the immediate exhortation of those who heard the prophet.
2. Prophecy utilizes poetic language filled with symbolic and figurative speech:
  a. Cosmic imagery is not necessarily the end of all space and time but likely the fall of a great nation (cf. Isa 13:9-11, cf. v. 1).
  b. For figurative language compare Isaiah 11:6-9 and 35:8-10.
3. Prophets often used theatrical enactments to get their point across (1 Kgs 22:29ff; Isa 20:1-4; Jer 27:2-3; Ezek 4:1ff; Acts 21:11). Sometimes their actions and even words can be crude.
4. Anthologies are collections of shorter units, often oral messages preached on a given occasion to a specific audience. These make some prophetic books particularly difficult to outline.
5. Indictment against Israel, especially for idolatry, religious ritualism, and social injustice.
6. Prophecy is almost always conditional. That is, the prediction is contingent upon Israel's response to God's message. If they repent, they will not be wiped out, or if they don't repent, the threats of God are fulfilled. Sometimes the word 'if' is included in conditional prophecy, sometimes it is merely assumed.
	1. Place the prophet within his time frame in Kings and Chronicles. Read what was going on politically and socially in the background of his prophecy.
	2. Don't expect precision with numbers, dates, or figures of speech. Prophecy is designed as an impassioned plea to contemporary repentance, not a scientific prediction of future events. You simply must allow, therefore, for ambiguity, paradox, and imprecision.
	3. Look for God's heart—sadness and sarcasm, especially in light of a broken covenant. These must be proclaimed pastorally yet forcefully in the light of contemporary social issues.
	4. Be cautious about using prophecy in apologetics. Some of the 'statistical' evidence of predictions proves to be artificial against closer hermeneutical scrutiny. But certainly, the OT prophets (and Psalms) do predict the coming of the Christ, and this is, at points, very compelling evidence of the foreknowledge and plan of God (John 5:39-47; Luke 24:18-19).
	5. Pay attention to the NT fulfillment of the OT, especially when actual texts are cited.
	6. Be humble and tentative with your eschatological conclusions.

#9 Apocalyptic: Ezekiel, Daniel, Zechariah, Matthew 24, 1 Thessalonians, Revelation
(This was a common genre from 100 B.C.E. to 100 C.E.)

Characteristics	Interpretive Rules
1. Hyperprophecy with rich symbolism and specific or even 'stock' phrases and vocabulary used commonly in Apocalyptic literature.	1. Since apocalyptic arises out of hopeless situations, it is intended for consolation of those who repent and fear for those who don't.
2. It often uses the literary device of a conversation between prophet/seer & God/angel, By seeing the world from this heavenly perspective, it allows Christians (or Jews) to persevere in their present suffering and to transform their reality through hope in Christ.	2. Rather than concentrating on figuring out the mysteries, first attempt to exhort the body of Christ to perseverance. Practical preaching is more important than 'cracking the code.'
3. One of the most common images is a cosmic catastrophe and imminent end of the age, resulting in radical transformation of all nature or nations in the near future.	3. Focus on the big picture: God is still in control. The future is certain and inextricably tied to the present: the choices you make now affect your eternal destiny.
4. Numbers should be weighed, not counted. Don't take them literally, but look for their symbolic meaning. For example 1 = unity, 2 = legal witness, 3 = divinity or supernatural power; 4 = humanity (4 winds), 7 = divine work on earth, 10 = completion. Likewise colors and objects (trumpets, horns, candles, etc.) are symbolic.	4. Pay attention to how the symbols are used in other prophetic literature. They are intertextual. That is, the symbols are clues that send you to another passage where that image is used and already understood. Take these figures seriously but not necessarily literally.
5. It combines multiple genres—letter, prophecy, poetry, etc. It is the most complex literary genre of the Bible because all the rules of all these genres apply.	5. Revelation is best understood not as a *calendar* of coming events, but rather as a *template* to be laid over a period of suffering to understand what is going on.
6. Like prophecy in general, it is christological and pastoral more than predictive and chronological.	

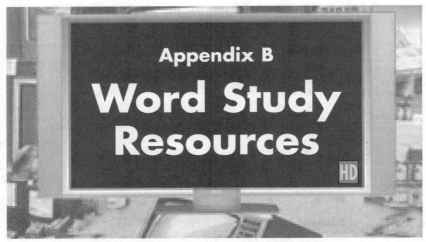

Appendix B
Word Study Resources
HD

Helps for Greek Word Studies

By Shawn Lindsay

*Represents works that are most helpful or even essential for N.T. word studies

Balz, H., and G. Schneider. *Exegetical Dictionary of the New Testament.* 3 vols. Grand Rapids: Eerdmans, 1990–1993. [R225.4803; E96]
> This is a popular-level resource with concise articles. The data is worthy of being called scholarly, yet readable. Consideration is given to usage prior to as well as within the NT. Words are arranged in order of the Greek alphabet, however, knowledge of Greek is not needed.

Bauer, Walter; William F. Arndt; and F. Wilbur Gingrich. *A Greek-English Lexicon of the New Testament and Other Early Christian Literature.* 2nd ed, rev. Chicago, University of Chicago Press: 1979. [R487.03; B344g]
> Among lexicons, Bauer-Arndt-Gingrich (BAG), is the standard. Words are in order by the Greek alphabet and are further defined by how they are used. This is a great resource for finding parallels (especially in the Bible) and references to Greek words used beyond the NT in early Christian writings. Most articles are very concise.

*Brown, Colin. *The New International Dictionary of New Testament Theology.* 3 vols. Exeter: Paternoster, 1980. [R225.3; N532]
> Colin Brown, or abbreviated *NIDNTT*, is a solid popular-level resource. Although it has scholarly depth, it is not as comprehensive as Kittel. Attention is given to the way the words were used in classical literature, in the LXX version of the OT, as well as in the NT. Words are arranged topically, so the student should refer to the index in volume 3 to search for: the Greek word, the transliterated Greek word, or by Scripture reference.

*Gilbrant, Thoralf. *The Complete Biblical Library.* [R220.07; C737]

> This 17-volume series is *the* most helpful resource for those with no knowledge of Greek. The series is divided into two sets. The first is a set of books that act as commentaries and a Greek-English interlinear for all of the NT books. The interlinear section shows each Greek word along with its English transliteration and a definition. In addition, the words are coded with a numbering system unique to the series.
>
> The second set of books are lexicons to the Greek words. These volumes serve as both dictionaries and concordances for the Greek word, not the English definition. A cross-reference is given for each word to various other noteworthy reference books. All words are parsed or declined in both the lexicons and in the interlinear in the first set of books.

Goodrick, E.W.; and John R. Kohlenberger III. *The NIV Exhaustive Concordance.* Grand Rapids: Zondervan, 1990. [R220.5208; G655n]

> This concordance is coded with the G/K numbering system but has conversion tables for cross-referencing with Strong's numbers. Each Greek word is listed by its G/K number in an appendix that tells the total number of uses of the word in the Greek NT and all its NIV synonyms. Knowledge of Greek is not needed.

Kittel, Gerhard. *Theological Dictionary of the New Testament.* 10 vols. Grand Rapids: Eerdmans, 1985. [R225.3; T391k]

> Kittel is *the* scholarly standard in Greek word studies (also known as *TDNT*). The voluminous footnotes allow for in-depth research. Consideration is given to use of the words in classical literature, the OT, the NT, and other nonbiblical works. Words are arranged according to the Greek alphabet with numerous other Greek words/phrases used throughout the definitions. A knowledge of the Greek language is essential. A one-volume abridged addition is also available [R225.480321; T391].

*Kohlenberger III, John R.; Edward W. Goodrick; James A. Swanson. *The Greek English Concordance to the New Testament.* Grand Rapids: Zondervan, 1997. [R225.48; K81g]

> Words are arranged alphabetically with the Greek as well as with the G/K numbering system. This volume is an excellent resource and very user-friendly to those with no knowledge of the Greek language who use the NIV Bible. Next to each entry, the number of times the English word is used in the NIV and in the Greek is given. Also, synonyms are listed by their G/K number next to each entry.

Kubo, Sakae. *A Reader's Greek-English Lexicon of the New Testament.* Berrien Springs, MI: Andrews University Press, 1971. [R487.03; K95r]

> This text will assist the student who is able to read from the Greek NT with the more difficult and/or less commonly used words. Included

with each word is a statistic of how many times a word is used within the book being studied as well as how many times the word appears in the NT.

Liddell, Henry G.; and Robert Scott. *A Greek-English Lexicon.* New York: Harper and Brothers, 1855. [R483.3; L712l]
>   Liddell & Scott is very close to BAG. Knowledge of Greek vocabulary is helpful. Many references to extrabiblical material are given.

Louw, Johannes P.; and Eugene A. Nida. *A Greek-English Lexicon of the New Testament Based on Semantic Domains.* New York: United Bible Society, 1989. [R487.4; G793]
>   The words and their brief definitions are arranged according to semantic range (i.e., categories of word usage). This makes it easy to find synonyms of words.

Moulten, W. F.; A. S. Geden; H. K. Moulten. *A Concordance to the Greek New Testament.* New York: T. & T. Clark, 2002. [R225.48;M927c]
>   This is *the* Greek concordance. This volume alleviates confusion of how words are translated in various versions of English Bibles by listing every entry in Greek. Thus, knowledge of the Greek language is essential.

Mounce, William D. *The Analytical Lexicon to the Greek New Testament.* Grand Rapids: Zondervan, 1993. [R487.4; M928a]
>   This is a more technical work that parses/declines every word in the Greek NT. This is an excellent resource for those with knowledge of the Greek language but should be used sparingly so as not to become a crutch.

Spicq, Ceslas. *Theological Lexicon of the New Testament.* 3 vols. Peabody, MA: Hendrickson, 1994. [R487.4; S754t]
>   This 3-volume series is very concise but not as scholarly. A knowledge of the Greek is not necessary; most words are transliterated into English. Extensive footnotes.

Thayer, Joseph H. *A Greek-English Lexicon of the New Testament.* Edinburgh: T. & T. Clark, 1908. [R483.2; T371g]
>   Thayer's lexicon has a wealth of biblical parallels. A knowledge of Greek vocabulary is helpful but not necessary.

Verbrugge, Verlyn D., ed. *The NIV Theological Dictionary of the New Testaments Words.* Grand Rapids: Zondervan, 2000. [R225.3; N532-2]
>   This is an abridgement of Colin Brown—superlative for a quick reference.

*Vine, W. E. *Vine's Expanded Expository Dictionary of New Testament Words.* Minneapolis: Bethany House, 1984. [R225.52033; V782v]

> Vine's is possibly the most popular among Greek dictionaries. This text is very readable; most all articles are quite short. Words are arranged topically and coded to Strong's numbers.

Helps for Hebrew Word Studies

(Arranged by Mark Moore)

Beall, Banks, and Smith. *Old Testament Parsing Guide.* 2 vols. Nashville: Broadman & Holman, 2000. [R 492.45;B3660]

> This is only helpful for those with a bit of Hebrew under their belt. It identifies the conjugations of Hebrew verbs. It is arranged verse by verse.

Botterweck, H., ed. *Theological Dictionary of the Old Testament.* 5 vols. Grand Rapids: Eerdmans, 1974. [R 221.3; B751]

> This is a "Kittel" for the OT. It is very thorough but technical.

Brown, F.; S. R. Driver; C. A. Briggs. *Hebrew-English Lexicon of the Old Testament* [BDB]. Oxford: Oxford University Press, 1997. [R 492.4321; G389n]

> This is *the* classic Hebrew Bible dictionary. The new version is keyed to Strong's, but still requires some knowledge of Hebrew to be used.

*Gilbrant, T. *The Complete Biblical Library* [R221.07;C737h]

> Start here for Hebrew word studies. It does what *The Complete Biblical Library* NT series does.

*Harris, R.; G. Archer; and B. Waltke. *Theological Wordbook of the Old Testament.* 2 vols. Chicago: Moody, 1980. [R221.3; H315]

> This is an extremely helpful resource for writing word studies, particularly with the range of meaning as well as derivatives and synonyms. Words are listed in Hebrew alphabetical order; however, there is an index in the back of volume two that is keyed to Strong's numbering.

*Kohlenberger, J. R.; and James A. Swanson. *The Hebrew English Concordance to the Old Testament.* Grand Rapids: Zondervan, 1998. [R221.44; K79h]

> This concordance lists in English every verse that contains a particular Hebrew word. It is alphabetized in Hebrew but is keyed to the NIV Concordance (Kohlenberger).

Owens, J. *Analytical Key to the Old Testament.* 4 vols. Grand Rapids: Baker Book House, 1989–1992. [R 221.44; O97a]
> This reference goes through the OT verse by verse analyzing the conjunctions and declensions of the Hebrew words. This is primarily helpful for those with a bit of Hebrew knowledge.

Unger, M.; and W. White. *Nelson's Expository Dictionary of the Old Testament.* Nashville: Thomas Nelson, 1980. [R 221.44; N431]
> This is a "Vine's" for the Old Testament. See also Vine, W. *An Expository Dictionary of Old Testament Words.* Old Tappan, NJ: Revell, 1978.

*Van Gemeren, W. *New International Dictionary of Old Testament Theology and Exegesis.* 5 vols. Grand Rapids: Zondervan, 1998. [R 221.3; N532]
> This is the equivalent to *NIDNTT* in the NT. It is an absolute *must* for word studies in the OT. It is particularly helpful with etymology and uses of the word outside the OT.

Westerman, Claus; and Ernst Jenni. *Theological Lexicon of the Old Testament.* 3 vols. Peabody, MA: Hendrickson, 1997. [R 221.447; T391]
> This goes beyond a mere dictionary in that it analyzes the theological import of the word beyond its lexical and etymological functions. However, one needs some familiarity with Hebrew grammar to make full use of this work.

Wigram, G. *Englishman's Hebrew-Chaldee Concordance.* Grand Rapids: Zondervan, 1972.
> This concordance lists in English every verse that contains a particular Hebrew word. It is alphabetized in Hebrew but is keyed to Strong's numbers.

Wilson, W. *New Wilson's Old Testament Word Studies.* Grand Rapids: Kregel, 1987. [R221.52033;W754n]
> Similar to Unger and Vine.

Appendix C
Website Annotated Bibliography

(Organized by Topic)

Audio Resources

🖱 http://www.audiotreasure.com/ (Found in *Chapter 2 — AIM*)
This website offers free downloads of multiple versions of the Bible for free. There are links that connect you to various websites where the downloads are available for free. You can then listen to the Bible through your computer, burn them to CD, or even put them on your iPod for your convenience. Immersing yourself in the word of God has never been easier.

🖱 http://markmoore.org/resources/lectures.html (Found in *Chapter 3 — Context*)
This aspect of Mark Moore's website is truly amazing and extremely useful for Bible study. This page offers all of Mark's lectures on the book of Acts (2 semesters), Principles of Interpretation, and Issues of Interpretation that he gives each year to Bible college students. This is literally a Bible college education offered to you for free. If you are interested in more resources like this one, Mark Moore is the president of the Institute for Christian Resources (ICR) which is dedicated to developing a digital seminary from the best Bible college professors around the nation. Check out more resources and opportunities to partner with ICR at: www.icrnet.org.

Bible Dictionaries

🖱 http://www.bible-history.com/smiths/ (Found in *Chapter 4 — History*)
This division of Bible History Online offers the entire *Smith's Bible Dictionary* for free. Like other online Bible dictionaries, this one is formatted in the convenient alphabetical order so that you simply have to click

173

on the letter that your topic of study begins with and you can read any available articles on your topic.

🖱 http://www.biblestudytools.net/Dictionaries/ (Found in *Chapter 4 — History*)
This section of the Cross Walk website offers a great launching pad to a small section of Bible dictionaries. While the selection may not be overwhelming, what is offered on this webpage *is* overwhelming. You can search *Baker's Evangelical Dictionary of Biblical Theology*, *Hitchcock's Bible Name Dictionary*, *Smith's Bible Dictionary*, and more. These tools are not easy to track down for free on the internet, but you get them all here at Cross Walk.

🖱 http://eastonsbibledictionary.com/ (Found in *Chapter 4 — History*)
No, this is no mistake. This website offers the entire *Easton's Bible Dictionary* online for free. Listed in alphabetical order, the dictionary is literally one click away. You can access any and all of the articles that are available through *Easton's Bible Dictionary* for your research needs.

🖱 http://www.eastons-bible-dictionary.com/eastons/bible-study.htm (Found in *Chapter 4 — History*)
The key advantage of this website is the search-engine feature. Instead of going through alphabetical lists of the articles found in *Easton's Bible Dictionary*, this website allows you to simply type in a word, phrase, or passage, and all of the articles where your request is found will come up in a Google-like format. This makes your research much more comprehensive with less effort.

🖱 http://studylight.org/dic/ (Found in *Chapter 2 — AIM*)
This link connects you to a hub of Bible dictionaries that are linked to places where you can access the half-dozen dictionaries listed. You can investigate the *American Tract Society Bible Dictionary*, the *Easton's Bible Dictionary*, the *Holman Bible Dictionary*, the *Hitchcock's Bible Names Dictionary*, the *King James Dictionary*, and the *Smith's Bible Dictionary*. This link is a part of a much larger website, studylight.org, which is full of great resources as well.

Bible Encyclopedias

🖱 http://www.christiananswers.net/dictionary/home.html (Found in *Chapter 4 — History*)
This is the Web Bible Encyclopedia. The site boasts over 4,100 articles and definitions for biblical study, once again organized in convenient alphabetical order. A strength and weakness of this site is the fact that it is constantly being updated with new and revised definitions and articles. This is a plus because you get up-to-date information, but this is a negative because you may want to pay attention to the credentials of the people

updating. Nevertheless, this is a great site for probing deeper in your biblical study.

🖰 http://www.studylight.org/enc/isb/ (Found in *Chapter 4 — History*)
This link connects you to the entire *International Standard Bible Encyclopedia* online for free. This resource is normally four thick volumes in hardback book, but here it is all online accessible in alphabetical order. You will find the depth of these articles to be extremely useful for more in-depth study than most Bible dictionaries offer.

Bibles

🖰 http://www.audiotreasure.com/ (Found in *Chapter 2 — AIM*)
This website offers free downloads of multiple versions of the Bible for free. There are links that connect you to various websites where the downloads are available for free. You can then listen to the Bible through your computer, burn them to CD, or even put them on your iPod for your convenience. Immersing yourself in the word of God has never been easier.

🖰 http://www.bible.org/page.php?page_id=3086 (Found in *Chapter 1 — Intro*)
This link takes you to a section of bible.org website, which is a site dedicated to connecting interested students to various resources and tools for theological study and training. The specific section of bible.org that this address takes you to is a place where you can download the NET Bible for free in a number of different formats.

🖰 http://www.discountchristian.com/freesoftware.html (Found in *Chapter 5 — Words*)
This link offers free biblical software that you can download for your computer or even your palm pilot. You can download Bibles, books, and many other resources for free from this site. Also, this site functions as a hub to a multitude of other computer resources that you can download for free or purchase, depending on the particular item located.

Biblical Archaeology

🖰 http://www.biblicalarcheology.net/ (Found in *Chapter 2 — AIM* and in *Chapter 4 — History*)
This website is in the blog format that gives you access to various articles, links, and even videos from experts focusing specifically on biblical archaeology. The extreme upside of this website is the consistent updating of the information on the website as more archaeological information is discovered. Furthermore, they have their blog entries archived on the left-hand side of the page based on topic for more convenient searches.

🖱 http://www.biblicalarchaeology.org/ (Found in *Chapter 2 — AIM* and in *Chapter 4 — History*)
The Biblical Archaeology Society (BAS) sponsors this website as their base of operations. The BAS is dedicated to examining, reporting, and utilizing the most up-to-date archaeological evidence to help re-create the biblical world for our interpretive endeavors. The BAS puts out the *Biblical Archaeology Review*, which is a magazine totally dedicated to archaeological finds that are pertinent to biblical study. This website will give you access to various articles, resources, and opportunities in biblical archaeology.

Biblical Articles

🖱 http://apmethodist.org/biblestudy.htm (Found in *Chapter 4 — History*)
This website offers another interesting, unique tool for biblical study that revolves around specific articles written on specific topics within specific books. The way you search the particular site is by book, which will then lead you to a section that contains various articles pertinent to the study of that particular book. You can find things from articles on theological issues to coins from the city of interest. This site spans both the Old and the New Testament.

🖱 http://markmoore.org/classes/principles/wordstudies.html (Found in *Chapter 4 — Words*)
This particular section of markmoore.org offers an assortment of the articles from Kenny Boles (Greek professor at Ozark Christian College in Joplin, MO) written on specific words in the New Testament. Each article is concise in its presentation, but each article is packed with enlightening presentations of New Testament words that can aid you in your study of a particular book or passage.

Biblical Culture/Customs

🖱 http://www.crivoice.org/historyculture.html (Found in *Chapter 2 — AIM*)
This link takes you to a webpage that connects you to a significant number of articles that focus on particular topics regarding certain cultural and historical issues you might encounter in biblical study. The topical articles are categorized under four sections: general, Old Testament, Intertestamental Period, and New Testament. While specific research on a particular topic may be difficult from this website, you can get a good feel for some of the pressing cultural/historical issues that contribute to biblical study.

🖱 http://www.middletownbiblechurch.org/biblecus/biblec.htm (Found in *Chapter 2 — AIM*)
This website is dedicated to research regarding biblical customs and culture. There are lengthy articles on various topics including: biblical meas-

urements, eating, clothing, transportation, farming, holidays, money, animals, and even plants/trees. You can get a wealth of information that allows you to piece together the everyday life of a typical person of the Bible.

Commentaries

http://www.biblestudytools.net/Commentaries/ (Found in *Chapter 4 — History*)
This website offers a decent selection of online commentaries that you can use in your study free of charge. You can tap into a variety of works, including: J.W. McGarvey's *Harmony of the Four Gospels*, the *Geneva Study Bible*, and even A.T. Robertson's *Word Studies on the Greek New Testament*. This source gives you a wide selection of commentary resources for your study.

http://cf.blueletterbible.org/commentaries/ (Found in *Chapter 4 — History*)
This webpage is a section of Blue Letter Bible. Specifically, this section of the website offers the textual commentaries of about 23 different authors, which include: John Calvin, Alfred Edersheim, Matthew Henry, J.B. Lightfoot, Martin Luther, and Charles Spurgeon. This is a great way to get a wide array of perspectives from different periods of time on a particular text.

http://www.mybibletools.com/bible/commentaries.htm (Found in *Chapter 4 — History*)
Using this tool, you can search for a topic or a passage in Bible commentary tools, specific commentary sets, and even sermons by people like Charles Spurgeon. The powerful search engine with the multiple tools gives this site obvious advantages to the careful researcher.

http://www.rickysoo.com/mhcc/ (Found in *Chapter 4 — History*)
This website gives you access to Matthew Henry's Concise Commentary . . . for free. This small commentary written by Henry in the 17th–18th centuries has blessed the church with exegetical insights for centuries. Each book of the Bible has comments on it by Henry on this website.

Concordances/Word Studies

http://bible.crosswalk.com/Concordances/NavesTopicalBible/ (Found in *Chapter 7 — Parallel Passages*)
This website gives you access to *Nave's Topical Bible* free of charge. The benefit of such a tool is specifically for word studies, in that you can search the entire resource by typing a word into the search engine. The results

present all of the references in the entire Bible in which that particular word is found. With a simple click, you can then read each of the contexts in which your word appears.

🖰 http://bible.gospelcom.net/bible
This is an online concordance. You can search for both words and passages in a broad variety of Bible translations.

🖰 www.eliyah.com/lexicon.html (Found in *Chapter 5 — Words*)
This website functions as a hub for powerful search engines that can help you in your biblical studies. The page has multiple areas for you to type in your topic or passage, in which the particular area utilizes a different search tool. For example, there are search tools for: Strong's concordance, Brown-Driver-Briggs' Hebrew Lexicon, Thayer's Greek Lexicon, Encarta Encyclopedia, or simply a search tool for the whole internet. This could be a powerful tool that allows you to study multiple avenues from the same webpage.

🖰 http://www.mybibletools.com/bible/word-study.htm (Found in *Chapter 5 — Words*)
This section of mybibletools.com is dedicated to offering a wide array of tools for biblical word studies. You can search for your particular word in multiple Bible translations simultaneously, the entire internet, sermons, Bible dictionaries, Bible encyclopedias, and even a Webster's thesaurus. In doing biblical word studies, you will not need much more than this website has to offer.

🖰 http://www.studylight.org/isb/ (Found in *Chapter 6 — Grammar*)
This powerful tool enables you to search for particular words in the entire Bible, in just a book of the Bible, or even in a verse of the Bible. The search results give you a broken down presentation of each verse in which your word appears, and the option to go further in defining the word with multiple help links for your study. This can be accomplished in English, Greek, and Hebrew. This is an incredible, free tool for Bible word studies.

General Bible Study Tools

🖰 www.biblestudytools.net (Found in *Chapter 3 — Context*)
This website, also referred to as crosswalk.com, is a great place for general Bible study in multiple areas of interest. The website offers a variety of avenues for study including: interlinear Bibles, commentaries, concordances, Bible dictionaries, sermon illustrations, and many other options from which to choose. It is a great place to start your research since there are so many elements offered in one place and at one time. It does not have the NIV or its tools, however. Furthermore, its Greek and Hebrew is all transliterated.

🖰 http://www.bibliapedia.com/ (Found in *Chapter 4 — History*)

This website has the potential to be an amazing site for biblical study. At the time of the writing of this book, a lot of the features for this site were still under construction, but the future possibility of what this will have to offer is astounding. There are portals for: free online encyclopedia with over 2,000 articles, ancient text library, online Bible with cross-references, free software downloads, daily Bible studies, and even a forum that offers an interactive community. Keep your eye on this site for future functionality, because this will be an incredible tool.

🖰 http://www.blueletterbible.org/index.html (Found in *Chapter 3 — Context* and in *Chapter 5 — Words*)

Blue-letter Bible is an amazing tool for biblical studies . . . for free. This website is amazing in its power and results. You can start off by simply typing a passage, topic, or phrase, and then Blue-letter Bible guides you to a wealth of information including: parallel passages, Greek/English concordance, selected commentaries, related hymns or images, maps, and dictionary aids. Another important feature is the ability to have about 13 different translations listed in parallel form for any verse or passage of your choice. The possibilities of this tool for biblical studies are virtually endless and invaluable.

🖰 http://www.carm.org/dresources.htm

This site contains an incredible array of links from apologetics to politics, from cults to theology.

🖰 http://gospeloutreach.net/bsr.html

Much of this site links to biblestudytools.net, but it is very cool and has an audio Bible that works with Real Player. Put your mouse on the bookshelf to see all the options available.

🖰 www.logos.com (Found in *Chapter 5 — Words*)

This is the website for the most powerful computer digital library that is in existence. Logos (or the Libronix Digital Library) offers many different packages to purchase that contain the tools to do any study that is referenced in this book. While the prices may seem extravagant, you can literally have entire commentary series, word study tools (Greek, Hebrew, and English), any number of books, and powerful search tools at your fingertips and everywhere you go. There is no more important computer tool for biblical study than the Logos system.

🖰 http://www.ntgateway.com/multibib.htm

This site offers a broad array of search abilities both in the biblical text and in resource materials and journals.

🖰 http://speedbibledictionary.com/ (Found in *Chapter 4 — History*)

This website offers a number of biblical study opportunities. While it offers searches through Bibles, Bible dictionaries, topical Bibles, Bible concordances, and many other study tools, it also offers the possibility of downloading these programs to your computer for use offline at a reasonable price. In addition, you can download "speaking Bibles," which allow you to hear the Bible in multiple languages aloud. There is also a section of free Bible software downloads with an assortment of options.

Hermeneutics Resources

http://hermeneutics.kulikovskyonline.net/hermeneutics/introherm.htm (Found in *Chapter 1 — Intro*)
This web page is a general overview of the purpose, tools, process, and further readings intricate to the interpretative process. This information is presented by Andrew S. Kulikovsky in a user-friendly manner that could serve as an important quick-reference for some of the hermeneutical principles expounded upon in this book.

http://home.comcast.net/~rciampa/ (Found in *Chapter 1 — Intro*)
In this website, Dr. Roy E. Ciampa gives a wealth of important resources for serious hermeneutic students. Ranging from links on writing exegesis papers to abbreviations of ancient literature to extensive bibliographies to original source access, Dr. Ciampa offers a virtual hub to an endless amount of resources and information. This is a great place to get connected to the deeper needs of biblical interpretation and study.

http://markmoore.org/classes/principles/ (Found in *Chapter 1 — Intro*)
This link connects you to Mark Moore's website, which you can explore to find other resources and opportunities to partner with Mark in biblical studies. This particular link takes you to the *principles of interpretation* section of his website. From this location, you can view the college syllabus used for the class offered that communicates this book on a college level. Furthermore, there are links on this page to helpful PowerPoint presentations, word studies by Kenny Boles, and even a list of essential readings for further hermeneutics study.

Maps

http://www.abideinchrist.com/messages/chronisr.html (Found in *Chapter 7 — Parallel Passages*)
This link offers a map of the entire Chronology of the Nation of Israel, presented by Wil Pounds. In timeline form, the website presents the Scripture references, Kings, time period, prophets, and foreign powers. This is a great visual presentation of this potentially confusing arrangement of people, times, and places in the Old Testament.

http://www.bible.ca/maps/ (Found in *Chapter 2 — AIM*)
This website offers free high-resolution maps. The site is somewhat limited in that it offers only about 26 different maps, but the quality of these maps

is great. There is a section of the webpage that offers various links to other places for some resources that may prove to be of some help to you in your various studies.

http://www.bible-history.com/maps/ (Found in *Chapter 2 — AIM* and in *Chapter 4 — History*)
This is a great website flooded with dozens of maps focusing on key cities, locations, and even time periods that impact biblical interpretation. The only downside of this website is the organization of the maps could be a little more user-friendly, but they are not lacking in their options. In addition, there are links on the side of the webpage that connect you with various other resources for further study.

http://www.biblemap.org/ (Found in *Chapter 2 — AIM* and in *Chapter 4 — History*)
This website offers biblical maps with a twist. There is a great interface at this link where you can type in any biblical reference (book and chapter), and then, the map will go to a Google earth location that matches with the reference you inserted. This is a great tool to see where the biblical locations are found in today's world.

http://www.biblestudy.org/maps/main.html (Found in *Chapter 2 — AIM*)
This link will take you to an amazing hub for biblical maps. You will find maps dedicated to the apostle Paul's missionary journeys, various Bible timelines, Old Testament maps, New Testament maps, Ancient Roman Empire maps, general world maps, and even biblical genealogy maps. If you are looking for ways to bring the Bible to life, exploring this website of important biblical maps will help you immensely.

http://earth.google.com/ (Found in *Chapter 4 — History*)
Google Earth is an amazing tool for modern-day map study. This program is literally satellite photographs of the entire earth that is updated continually. You can literally type in an address and zoom in so close that you can see cars parked in driveways. This is a great tool for comparative studies of the terrain of the ancient world compared to the development of the same terrain in today's society. Can you find your house?

http://skylardesign.com/clients/oldsites/holman/assets/pdfs/bstudies/chart-of-kings.pdf (Found in *Chapter 7 — Parallel Passages*)
This link offers an extremely helpful chart that lines out every king reigning in each area of the divided kingdom along with the corresponding prophets set out on a timeline. In addition, the ruling empire is mapped out on the bottom of the page so that you can see what king reigned and what prophet spoke during the reign of the Assyrians, Babylonians, or the Persians. This is a great tool to use for Old Testament studies.

⌐ http://visibleearth.nasa.gov/view_set.php?categoryID=2116 (Found in *Chapter 4 — History*)

Similar to Google Earth, this website is a catalogue of satellite photographs taken from NASA themselves. While this is not as interactive as Google Earth, it is still extremely useful for still-frame research to show the comparative development of the terrain from the ancient times to the present condition of it.

Original Sources

⌐ http://www.bibletexts.com/ (Found in *Chapter 4 — History*)

While this website is another one that offers access to original texts of church history, the organization of the material is quite unique. You are able to search the church historians based on modern day explosive issues like: nonviolence, adultery, divorce, pornography, and even men/women issues. When you click on one of the topics, you will get biblical passages and church history selections that pertain to the topic you selected.

⌐ http://www.ccel.org/fathers.html (Found in *Chapter 4 — History*)

This incredibly powerful tool connects you with the writings of virtually every church father from whom we have writings. This particular link offers the writings of the Ante-Nicene Fathers, St. Augustine, St. Chrysostom, and the Nicene and Post-Nicene Fathers. To have all of these writings for free and at your fingertips is truly amazing.

⌐ http://www.earlyjewishwritings.com/philo.html (Found in *Chapter 4 — History*)

This link takes you to the complete writings of Philo. This important source for biblical study gives you a prominent Jewish philosopher's perspective on many Jewish texts and issues. Furthermore, when you click on any of the sources you are also given a short commentary and introduction to each section, which is quite convenient to help guide you through what you are reading.

⌐ http://www.iclnet.org/

This is the Internet Christian Library, containing a broad array of material. Of particular interest is the Early Church Documents on the Internet. Scroll down to find links to the church fathers, creeds, canons, etc. Full text is available.

⌐ http://www.jewishvirtuallibrary.org/jsource/Talmud/talmudtoc.html (Found in *Chapter 4 — History*)

The Jewish Talmud is found in its entirety on this website. Each section is initiated with a short introduction to the Talmudic material to find. This is great material that gives you insight into the Jewish perspectives and minds of the ancient world. This is an important document in the Jewish tradition, and likewise for Christians this resource can be great for biblical background study.

🖱 http://pace.cns.yorku.ca/York/york/texts.htm (Found in *Chapter 4 — History*)
This link connects you to two key original sources for biblical studies: Polybius and Flavius Josephus. When you click on one of the links for their works, you are guided to another page that shows the desired text in its original Greek with the parallel English translation right next to it. This convenience of reading the original sources even in their original languages is vital for biblical background study.

🖱 http://www.perseus.tufts.edu/cache/perscoll_Greco-Roman.html (Found in *Chapter 4 — History*)
This link connects you with the most powerful online resource for original source research. Perseus gives you access to virtually every piece of literature in the ancient world and their original languages. This is the first place that you should look when you are doing any sort of original source research. It is a very powerful tool for study.

🖱 http://www.sacred-texts.com/jud/tmm/index.htm (Found in *Chapter 4 — History*)
This link will connect you to a page called "Tales and Maxims from the Midrash." This page gives you access to the part of the Talmud that is referred to as the Midrash. In essence this is a Jewish commentary on various books of the Old Testament that was taken from oral tradition and put into written form. This will include a lot of "this rabbi said" and "this rabbi said" about the particular text being commented on.

🖱 http://www.targum.info/pj/psjon.htm (Found in *Chapter 4 — History*)
This website gives you access to two important targum families: Targum Pseudo-Jonathan and Targum Onkelos. The translations of all of the material are based on J.W. Etheridge's 1862 published work. The Targums both cover the Pentateuch in their comments and reflection.

🖱 http://torreys.org/bible/
A gateway focusing on early Christian writings and their social world.

🖱 http://wesley.nnu.edu/biblical_studies/noncanon/apocrypha.htm (Found in *Chapter 4 — History*)
This is a part of an entire website that is dedicated to original sources including works of John Wesley, Charles Wesley, and various others. In particular, this link will take you to the section of the website dedicated to Old Testament Apocryphal literature. In addition to the text of the Apocryphal literature, the website provides an introduction and a summary for each of the works.

🖱 http://wesley.nnu.edu/biblical_studies/noncanon/pseudepigrapha.htm (Found in *Chapter 4 — History*)
Once again, this is a part of an entire website that is dedicated to original sources including works of John Wesley, Charles Wesley, and various others. This link, however, will take you to the section of the website dedicated to the Old Testament Pseudepigrapha. In addition to the text of the Pseudipigraphical literature, the website provides an introduction and a summary for almost all of the works. Furthermore, some of the works are given in multiple versions for your convenience.

Photo Resources

🖱 http://freestockphotos.com/ (Found in *Chapter 4 — History*)
This website provides a whole slew of photographs that you can use to visualize some of the key elements in biblical background studies. The categories included in this website of stock photos include pictures of: animals, Christian related sites, Egypt, Israel, the Near East, plants, Rome, weather, and even various scenery photographs.

🖱 http://www.md.huji.ac.il/vjt/ (Found in *Chapter 4 — History*)
This website is entitled "Virtual Jerusalem Tour." As the title betrays, this website is full of modern photographs of significant sites and locations in Jerusalem. This is a great way to point to the exact locations in which various events probably occurred as recorded in the New Testament. This allows you to put a visual image in place of a nebulous reference to a particular region or place in the city of Jerusalem found in the Bible.

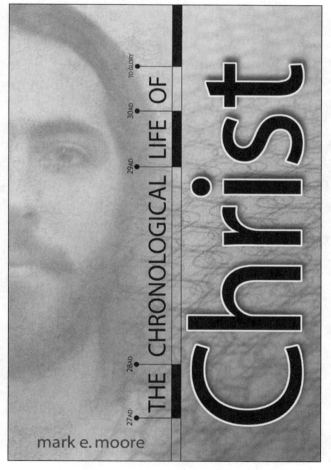

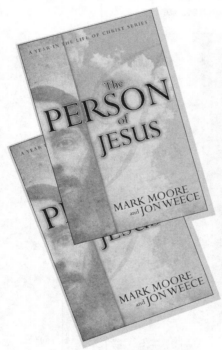
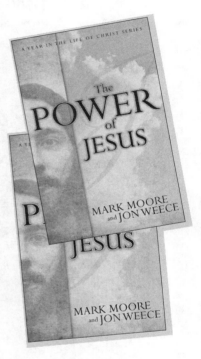

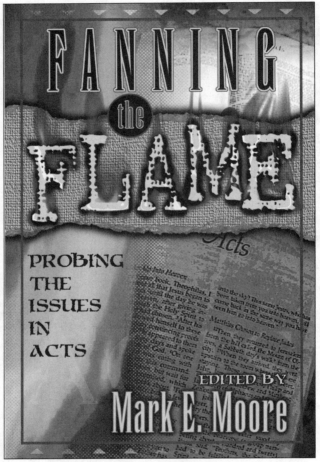

Mark Moore Takes on the Book of Revelation in His Inimitable Style

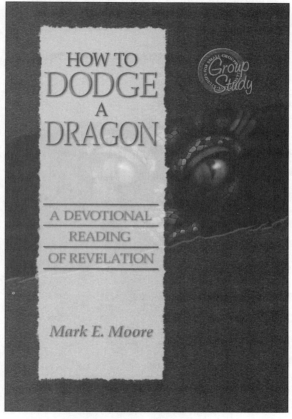

How to Dodge a Dragon
A Devotional Reading of Revelation
88 pages, soft bound
ISBN # 828-3

Coming Summer 2008

Perfect to use with youth or college students
in their small group or discipleship groups.
(May not reflect actual cover design)

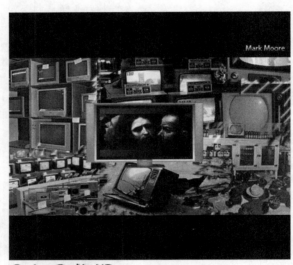

Seeing God in HD: Student Edition
soft cover